THE POET DONNE

THE POET DONNE

A STUDY
IN HIS DIALECTIC METHOD

by

UNA NELLY, M.A.

'He knew the anguish of the marrow.'
T. S. ELIOT

CORK UNIVERSITY PRESS

First published 1969

© *Cork University Press 1969*

Printed in the Republic of Ireland
by Hely Thom Limited, Dublin

CONTENTS

PR
2248
N4

8·25·72

'On a huge hill,
Cragged, and steep, Truth stands, and hee that will
Reach her, about must, and about must goe;
And what the hills suddennes resists, winne so;
Yet strive so, that before age, deaths twilight,
Thy soule rest . . .'

(Satyre III)

INTRODUCTION

IN A letter to Sir Henry Wotton, Donne makes the remark that

> 'both hearers and players are more delighted with voluntary than
> with sett musike'.

In choosing to write about the dialectic—or the method of logical
argumentation—which is the outstanding characteristic of his poetry
and of his prose works, I am following my own delight, and I hope
the delight of the hearers, in attending to Donne's 'voluntary', because
within its compass one can hear his very voice and in its discords and
concords discover the pattern of the living dialectic of his own inner
life. Reading his poems we are never mere passive lookers-on, but
feel ourselves within the crowded 'parvis' of Donne's mind and heart,
sharing the unique experience of seeing live thoughts and emotions
in the very moments of their formation, rise to take part as 'respondents' and 'opponents', in the vibrantly personal disputation to which
Donne's strongly dualistic nature readily lent itself, and where his
equally strong sense of reality sat as judge to analyse and resolve all
arguments. Of his poetry it could be said, in the words of another
great poet of individuation, G. M. Hopkins, that it

> Deals out that being indoors each one dwells;
> Selves—goes itself; myself it speaks and spells;
> Crying what I do is me: for that I came . . .

For Donne is intensely alive in the pulsating dialectic of his verse;
revealing new facets of his brilliant intellect, new shades of his rich
nature, as he endlessly investigated the truth; disputing with himself,
criticizing his motives, analysing his states of being, of feeling, of
knowing; satirizing whatever in thoughts or behaviour or events was
false or bogus.

But is the dialectical structure, and tone, of his verse—per se—the
distinguishing mark of Donne? Some of his outstanding critics seem
to think so. Grierson was the first to draw attention to the dialectical
strain in the love poetry;[1] Leishman goes further and considers 'the

---

[1] H. J. C. Grierson, *Poems of John Donne*, Vol. II, 1912, Intro.

dialectical expression of personal drama' a far more apt description of Donne's work than the term 'metaphysical' which is usually applied to it;[2] and Mario Praz, appraising Donne against his European background, does not hesitate to state that

> The chief thing with Donne is not the 'concetti' ... it is the dialectical slant of his mind.[3]

Helen Gardner and Allen Tate, while insisting on the dialectic (in their words, the method of argument or of logical reasoning), include imagery in their definitions of metaphysical poetry, H. Gardner claiming that

> argument and persuasion, and the use of the conceit as their instrument, are the elements or body of a metaphysical poem ...;[4]

while Tate states that

> The development of imagery by logical extension, the reasonable framework being an Ariadne's thread that the poet will not permit us to lose, is the hallmark of the poetry called metaphysical.[5]

The 'hallmark' and the 'elements' are not yet the essence, however, and, as W. H. Gardner remarks of the poems of Hopkins, it is the essence that counts. Essence has to do with life force, energizing power. We have to ask ourselves what is the driving force behind the dialectic of Donne's verse and sermons, and indeed of all his works? What prevents his poems from becoming mere pyrotechnic displays of wit, or verbal battles in pseudo-logic? What is it that endows the dialectic with the pliancy of living thought, the resonance of Donne's very voice, and above all, with the urgency that bespeaks his sincerity?

It will be my endeavour to examine whether it was Donne's consistent hunger for what is real and true, which energized and inflamed his dialectic. For Donne felt instinctively that God, being Himself the

---

[2] J. B. Leishman, *The Monarch of Wit*, 1962, p. 85.
[3] M. Praz, *A Garland for John Donne*, ed. T. Spencer, 1931 'Donne's Relation to the Poetry of his time,' p. 57.
[4] *The Metaphysical Poets*, Intro., p. 21.
[5] *On the Limits of Poetry*, N.Y., 1948, p. 80.

'summum Bonum', made man capable of coming into contact with
reality, not to evade it in dreams, to cover it up with pleasing façades,
nor to falsify it by unreal standards. It is of course true, as T. S. Eliot
remarks in 'Murder in the Cathedral', that

> ... human kind
> cannot bear very much reality ...

and that is why Donne is such a great poet—because he takes a hard
look at reality: the reality of his own complex emotional and intellectual life, as well as that of the human situation in which he finds
himself. The dialectic which rings through his poems and sermons can
be seen as a kind of Odyssey of the spirit, its real meaning lying in
Donne's attempt to reach ultimate reality, ultimate truth in God, in
order to attain to fullness of being, and to a sense of oneness with
reality from which the dualism of his nature held him back.

It is interesting to trace the sources of the dialectic habit in Donne;
first of all from the nature of the man himself; then, from the environment and the times into which he was born; and finally, from the
influences on his young manhood, particularly the strongly formative
influence of his education at Oxford University, from 1584 to 1587.
The curriculum at sixteenth century Oxford has been studied in some
detail because of my conviction that the dialectical and Aristotelian
qualities which still chiefly characterised it, played a major part in
developing innate tendencies in young John Donne. And influences
bespeak affinities.

Extracts from the *Elegies, Satyres, Songs and Sonets* and the *Divine
Poems,* as well as from the sermons all demonstrate the variety of ways
in which Donne employs the dialectic method—but always to the
one purpose: to discover and express reality.

> I thought, he remarks in the Preface to *Biathanatos*, that as in the
> poole of Bethsaida, there was no health till the water was troubled,
> so the best way to finde the Truth . . . was to debate and vexe
> it . . .[6]

Wit, in T. S. Eliot's sense of a certain 'tough reasonableness': honesty,
clear-sightedness, a sense of the real—this was Donne's supreme gift,
used by him to uncover the shams and reveal man in the human con-

---

[6] *Complete Poetry and Selected Prose*, ed. J. Hayward, 1945, p. 422.

dition, *as he is*. I have tried to show how Donne used the metaphysical image in a strictly logical manner, as the tool for his dialectic exploration of reality; how his adherence to the truth of things as they are, is reflected in the complexities, the tensions, and the rich ambiguities of his verse; how the duality in the structure of his nature combined with his conception of dialectic to lead him to seek truth in a balanced attitude between extremes of contrast; and above all, how his pre-adherence to God—Ultimate Reality, Truth Itself—gave his verse from the beginning the strain of a spiritual quest, the urgency of a deeply-felt personal dilemma, the dynamism of a being in contact with its Cause.

'Wit, play of intellect, stress of cerebral muscle' take the place in these poems of 'poetique rage', and 'the lazie seeds of servile imitation . . .' Behind the tender lover of the *Songs and Sonets*, the arrogant rebel of the *Elegies*, the cynical renegade of the *Satyres*, the clever satiriser of contemporary manners, and the 'true God's priest', we find, consistently, the challenging intellectual honesty, the unchanging spiritual aspiration of the living Donne.

'The world that I regard is myself; it is the Microcosm of my own frame that I cast mine eye on . . .'

Sir Thomas Browne: *Religio Medici*

CHAPTER I

THE MICROCOSM OF THE SELF

IT COULD be said with truth that John Donne himself is the living symbol for the dialectic, which such eminent critics of his work as Grierson, Leishman and Mario Praz, consider the outstanding characteristic of his poetry, because in his life and person one is all the time conscious of the tension produced by opposing elements, whether of events or opinions, whether in matters concerning the heart, or in crises confronting his rare and keen intelligence. The great virtue of his poetry lies in the fact that it possesses the intensity, the existential stress of life itself.

'For those who have experienced, or at least understand, the ups-and-downs, the ins-and-outs of human temperament,' writes Saintsbury, 'the alterations not merely of passion and satiety, but of passion and laughter, of passion and melancholy reflection, of passion earthly enough and spiritual rapture almost heavenly, there is no poet and hardly any writer like Donne.[1]'

The main sources for the few details we have of Donne's early years are: Walton's *Life*, published nine years after Donne's death, and the scattered autobiographical remarks which are to be found throughout his works.

John Donne was born in London, in 1572, in the hey-day of Elizabethan power. His parents were staunch Catholics, adhering loyally to the old faith despite threats and persecutions. Of his father we know little, except that he filled the office of warden to the Company of Ironmongers, and died when young John was but four years old. On his mother's side he was descended from noble and worthy stock. Daughter of John Heywood, the noted epigrammatist, composer of Interludes, gifted actor and musician, and sister to two famous Jesuits, Elias and Jasper Heywood, Donne's mother, Elizabeth, could claim a still nobler lineage in her direct descent from Thomas More, gentle

---

[1] G. Saintsbury, 'Introduction' to *Poems of John Donne*, ed., E. K. Chambers, 1896, Vol I, p. xxxii.

martyr and scholar of European renown; and from the Rastalls, that family of noted lawyers and judges, and loyal upholders of the old faith, into which Thomas More's sister had married.

The blood of martyrs, the thews of men of dedication, as well as the tenacity of lawyers and the genius of men of letters made up the natural inheritance of our poet, the rich tradition into which he was born and which moulded his soul and spirit during those impressionable years of his childhood and early boyhood. A sad childhood it must have been; listening at the age of six or seven to the fearful whisperings of his elders when his Jesuit uncle, Elias, secretary to Cardinal Pole of Tridentine fame, died in banishment for his loyal adherence to the Catholic cause; and again in the sensitive adolescent years, when the notoriety of the arrest and imprisonment of his second Jesuit uncle, Jasper, made his family still more suspect. What fear-laden memories, what nights haunted by unknown terrors are buried in that tell-tale admission made years later by Donne in his Preface to *Biathanatos* (1608):

> I had my first breeding and conversation with men of a suppressed and afflicted religion, accustomed to the despite of death, and hungry of an imagin'd Martyrdome.[2]

The years from 1582 to 1593 were years of the greatest persecution for those who clung to the old faith. Act after act was passed to terrorize the timid into conformity, and to penalize, even to the ignominy of the gallows, the gallant few who remained faithful.

During that sensitive period of his boyhood, Donne and his younger brother Henry, who with him occupied the central position in a family of four daughters and two sons, must have drawn very close to one another, particularly after the death, in 1583, of their eldest sister, Elizabeth. Then for three further years, the brothers shared the intimate joys and woes of undergraduate life at Oxford, and it is probable that they went abroad together in the years between 1587 and 1592, when Tyburn became a river of blood for Oxford men as gently nurtured and greatly gifted as Campion and his fellows. When did the brothers reach a parting of the ways? When did the reckless heroism of the martyrs invade the spirit of the younger brother, leading him at last to a damp

---

[2] *Complete Poetry & Selected Prose*, ed. J. Hayward, 1945, p. 420.

   Note: This is the edition of Donne's poems used throughout. Hereinafter it will be referred to as *Poetry & Prose*, Hayward.

death in Clink prison for the crime of harbouring a priest? From what foreign source did the motive spring which influenced Donne to leave the narrow way of the old religion, so full of hidden snares, for the broad, safe way of the royal religion? Was it this culminating grief of his only brother's needless death that broke at last the high courage and the tradition of loyalty he had inherited, in a family accustomed to count as glory the hardships and injustices they were called upon to bear in the cause of religion?

We shall never know the answers to these questions—except in so far as we can detect in Donne's poems and works a faintly elegiac note, or trace his growing sense of the vanity of all things earthly. With Grierson, and other historians of Donne, we must conclude that whatever the nature of the crisis which Donne underwent after his brother's death in 1593, he had at least outwardly conformed before 1597, when he was appointed secretary to Sir Thomas Egerton, later Lord Ellesmere, Keeper of the Great Seal and Lord High Chancellor of England.

It is the opinion of many eminent students of Donne that he was never wholly at ease in the Anglican Church. Whatever his motives, Donne could not but have seen the tranference of his allegiance as a kind of betrayal: a rejection of higher, other-worldly values in favour of lesser motives dictated—maybe—by ambition, self-preservation, all that is implied in the 'lust of the eyes and the pride of life'. Perhaps it was this consciousness of the implications of his choice which first brought home to him, in startling clarity, the dualism of his own nature. He had served his apprenticeship to Aristotle in the academic disputations at Oxford; he had applied himself to the study of law and the devious ways of lawyers at Thavies Inn, and later, from 1592 to 1596, at Lincoln's Inn; he had mastered the art of the apologist, having, he tells us

> survayed and digested the whole body of Divinity, controverted betweene ours and the Romane Church.[3]

but all these were but 'shadow-boxing' in comparison with the very real war which Donne was to wage within the centre of his being, between the flesh and the spirit, the head and the heart, the intelligence and the senses, the passions and the will, and which was to give to his poetry the distinguishing characteristic of a living argument, of a passionately, vibrant dialectic, in which Donne is at once 'Respondent'

---

[3] Preface to *Pseudo-Martyr*, 1610.

and 'Opponent', or in his calmer moods, wise 'Moderator', or waggish 'Terrae Filius'.[4]

Donne's inward, personal drama is markedly externalized in many of his poems, some of which we will examine briefly here.

We can easily recognize the debater's opening device of an abrupt personal attack in *The Sunne Rising*, and in *The Canonization*; the almost legal cross-examination of motives in *Womans Constancy*; the scholastic probing of detail, and the objective handling of a rarefied theme in *Aire and Angels*; the undergraduate humour in so many of the *Elegies*; the lively pitting of opinions, one against the other, in *The Canonization*, which is perhaps the most perfect example of the subtle manoeuvrings of the skilled disputant; and the delightfully personal argument of *The Blossome* where Donne's intelligence

> which lov'st to bee
> Subtile to plague (it)selfe

joins forces with his 'naked thinking heart', to contend with his bodily senses in a pulsating dialogue, which, I think, is far more convincing than the urbane and detached tone in Marvell's *A Dialogue between the Soul and Body*, or the over-dramatized version of Yeats's *A Dialogue of Self and Soul*.

In the *Song and Sonets*, where Donne's authentic voice is perhaps most clearly heard, it is easy to pick out and to label the various 'Respondents' and 'Opponents' which dramatize the particular interior conflict with which he was concerned. Donne's best poems include those in which he tries to resolve—or at least attain a precarious balance between—the conflicting forces, emotional and intellectual, of his own soul. His selection of reality is restricted, being confined in the main to that dark mysterious world which borders on the subconscious, that no-man's-land where body and spirit meet for the fleeting moment of an ecstasy, and where the white light of conscience shows us up suddenly and sharply for the cowards we are, and the perjurers we can become in our own defence.

Donne's 'other self' appears in the arguments under different guises: in *The Canonization* it speaks in the forceful voice of commonsense, deriding the folly of the lovers, while in *The Sunne Rising* its arguments are quickly dismissed by the complacent couple . . .

---

[4] For explanation of terms see Chap. III.

compar'd to this
All honor's mimique . . .
Nothing else is.

Loves Alchymie shows us an exasperated and cynical Donne giving voice—more or less as an exercise in exorcism—to the extremes of love, the idealized and the grossly carnal, to both of which he can discover aspirations in the dark mazy labyrinth of his own mind and soul.

Very often when his object is to explore the mysterious and contradictory character of the human heart in love—its fickleness and facile excuses (as in *Womans Constancy*); its possessiveness (*Lovers Infinitenesse*); its brutality (*The Apparition*)—he addresses his verses to a supposed mistress only to externalize and thus resolve his quandary. Most critics agree that his love poems cannot be regarded as autobiographical, with the exception perhaps of *A Valediction: forbidding mourning*, which Walton tells us Donne wrote for his wife before setting out for Paris with Sir Robert Drury, in 1611. These love poems will be examined in greater detail in Chapter V. Here I shall consider only *The Blossome* which is very typical of Donne, both in its subject matter and in the subtle play of its argument.

The Blossome

Donne was always more imaginatively engaged by the almost infinitely varied activity of the mind, its problems and poses and pretexts, the rise and the peculiar curve of its thought, than by the less varied and more stereotyped expressions of the passions. Here, in *The Blossome*, we have a poetic dramatization of the inner dialectic taking place in the crowded forum of Donne's mind, with the 'Respondent' and 'Opponent' taking the parts, respectively, of his heart and his senses.

We note the gently lyric opening, the analogy of the frail blossom with his wayward heart setting the tone of the poem, which is that of an indulgent parent towards a cherished child whom he sees deluded by appearances, and lulled into a false security which blinds it to the harsh realities of life:

Little think'st thou, poore flower,
Whom I have watch'd sixe or seaven dayes,
And Seene thy birth . . .

And now dost laugh and triumph on this bough,
Little think'st thou
That it will freeze anon, and that I shall
To morrow finde thee falne, or not at all.

In the second stanza, addressed directly to his heart, Donne mocks its
folly in expecting to find a permanent resting place in any human love:

Little think'st thou poore heart
That labour'st yet to nestle thee . . .
In a forbidden or forbidding tree . . .

The tone is still that of compassionate remonstrance when, at the end of
stanza two, he declares that this dalliance must cease; that, to-morrow,
before the mistress his heart now pays court to is awake, it must bow
to the exigencies of time and nature, and accompany his body back to
London.

With stanza three there is a marked change in tone and rhythm as
the forces are joined, and the heart 'which lov'st be bee/Subtile . . .'
speaks its part:

Alas, if you must goe, what's that to mee?
Here lyes my businesse, and here I will stay:

Dismissing the body with a fine contempt, it says 'You goe to friends
. . .'—who will satisfy its sensual appetites, and so leave the heart to
settle its own affairs, with the implication that these, of course, are of a
rare and suprasensory nature. In this way Donne wittily and dramatically depicts for us the age-old battle between the two extremes of
our nature: the ultra-idealistic which discounts the real, and the merely
carnal and sensual which is less than human. Later in this study we shall
see that this exploring and championing of the real, the truth in the
human condition, is the constantly recurring aim of Donne's free-
ranging and probing dialectic. Very often when he seems most flippant
he is in fact most serious. We note, for instance, in the final stanzas of
this poem, his criticism of values which are false to the human situation.
His condemnation of platonic love is implicit in:

A naked thinking heart, that makes no show,
Is to a woman, but a kinde of ghost.

While the other extreme of lust is censured in the final lines of the same stanza:

> How shall shee know my heart; or having none,
> Know thee for one? . . .

These stanzas of *The Blossome* are very typical of Donne, embodying many of the distinctive qualities of his verse. We note the colloquial terms which set the tone of intimacy; the broken, staccato rhythm suggesting the drama within; the subtlety of thought, the risqué quality of the wit, the conciseness of expression, and the perfect harmony of thought and structure leading to the climactic, and for Donne, the highly characteristic ending. Having agreed to the experiment, to this chosen frolic of his heart, he enjoins it to meet him—and note the concrete detail which gives a sense of immediacy and conviction to the experience:

> Meet me at London, then,
> Twenty dayes hence . . .

> I would give you
> There, to another friend, whom wee shall finde
> As glad to have my body, as my minde.

There is a whole world of difference between this poem of Donne's and the *Dialogues* of Marvell and of Yeats which, though cleverly constructed, seem too artificial and unreal with their rhetorical exclamations and questions:

> Oh who shall me deliver whole,
> From bonds of this Tyrannic Soul? . . .
>
>   *Marvell*

or, the dejected resignation of:

> I am content to live it all again . . .
> A blind man battering blind men . . .
>
>   *Yeats*

It is Donne's healthy attitude towards reality, towards wholeness in love, together with his intimate knowledge of the workings of the human heart, which give to his poem the variety and flow of life itself: the certainty of the frailty and impermanence of all things (so aptly symbolized by the blossom) lightened by the beauty of the lyric interludes or the fun of the occasional spree, and made bearable by the wit which accepts good humouredly, the imbalance, the self deceptions, and even the perverse desires of our nature.

All the dialectic in his poems, all the taking apart and analysing, all the thrust and parry of argument and counter-argument, all the effort implied in 'about must, and about must goe', not only reflects the state within, but is directed rather towards the attainment of the 'unified sensibility' with which T. S. Eliot has credited Donne, than an evidence that he has attained to such. His distinctive use of the image of the microcosm suggests the satisfying wholeness and security, denied him in his fear-ridden childhood and youth, sought by him always, and found—temporarily at any rate—in true and mutual love:

> Let us possess one world, each hath one, and is one.
> *The Good Morrow*

Such security Donne found in the love of Ann More, the niece of Lady Egerton, whom he married secretly in 1601. But, as we shall see, there was to be no lasting rest for his questing heart, no easy resolution of the dichotomies of his nature in any merely human love.

The years of his great unrest, between 1593 and 1601, were the years which saw the creation of his best and most original work in the *Songs and Sonets*, the *Elegies* and the *Satyres*. It seems as if struggle and doubt were the necessary concomitants of his inspiration, and bear out the remark of Yeats:

> We make out of the quarrel with others, rhetoric, but of the quarrel with ourselves, poetry . . . we sing amid our uncertainty.[5]

Donne's comment, in a letter to his friend, Sir Henry Goodyer (1608) on this characteristic of his nature, is both striking and revealing:

> I would not that death should take me asleep. I would not have him meerly seise me, and onely declare me to be dead, but win me, and overcome me. When I must shipwrack, I would do it in a

---

[5] W. B. Yeats, *Anima Hominis*, p. 45.

Sea, where mine impotencie might have some excuse; not in a
sullen weedy lake, where I could not have so much as exercise
for my swimming.[6]

And in *Satyre III* we have his poetic apologia in lines, which by their
very structure and rhythm, suggest the incessant straining after truth,
the persevering, dogged effort of his keenly-searching dialectic:

> On a huge hill
> Cragged and steep, Truth stands, and hee that will
> Reach her, about must, and about must goe;
> And what the hills suddennes resists, winne so . . .

This is a poem about Donne's search for Truth, and when we remember that it was written in 1593, the year in which he lost his brother,
Henry, and moreover, that he himself was then only in his twenty-first
year, we must marvel at the maturity and the balance of mind which
it reveals.

Whether Donne in these disturbed times did not wish to adhere to
any particular Church, preferring 'God Himselfe to trust'; or whether
his vision did indeed go beyond petty differences of sects to a greater
truth which transcended, yet included them all; or whether, and this
seems the most likely supposition, he is here crying out against the
extremes which destroy—the extreme of martyrdom which, in his
experience, seemed the exorbitant price one must now pay for adhering to the Roman Church, and the extreme of irresponsibility which
prompted so many to accept uncritically, almost blindly, the tenets of
any sect which could serve their cause—whatever the case, he is insistent
in the Satyre to:

> Seeke true religion . . .

> Though truth and falsehood bee
> Neare twins, yet truth a little elder is;
> Be busie to seeke her . . .

Then follows his plea for the 'via media':

> To adore, or scorne an image, or protest,
> May all be bad; doubt wisely; in strange way
> To stand inquiring right, is not to stray;
> To sleepe, or runne wrong, is.

---

[6] *Poetry & Prose*, Hayward, op. cit., p. 455.

To 'doubt wisely' could be regarded as Donne's life-long motto. Hence in his poems we find the endless interrogating of his motives, the clash of opinion against opinion, the frequent turning back upon his line of thought, the tenuous balance which is so often the outcome of all his strenuous dialectic, the truce, as it were, between the extremes of his nature, where the hero and the coward struggle for the mastery.

In another letter to Sir Henry Goodyer written in April 1615, fifteen months after his ordination as an Anglican clergyman, the doubts and the unease still persist:

> You shall seldome see a Coyne, upon which the stamp were re-moved, though to imprint it better, but that it looks awry and squint. And so, for the most part, do mindes which have received divers impressions. I will not, nor need you, compare the Relig-ions. The channels of God's mercies run through both fields; and they are sister teats of his graces, yet both diseased and infected, not both alike . . .[7]

Here there is no evidence that Donne had pursued his own advice to 'seek true religion', since to him both Churches seem 'diseased'. Some three years later he composed the *Holy Sonnet XVIII* in which he prays:

> Showe me, deare Christ, thy Spouse . . .

asking for a definite sign whereby he might know her beyond doubt. Of this poem Grierson shrewdly remarks:

> This is not the language of one who is walking in the via media with the intellectually untroubled confidence of Herbert.[8]

Intellectually troubled Donne must have been if it was mere worldly prudence, alien to his nature and upbringing, which prompted him to abandon a persecuted, outlawed Church in pursuit of high office and the favours of the great. One can see a veritable dialectic demonstrated in the events of his life: this cold worldly prudence disputing with, and triumphing over the natural loyalty of his passionate nature, only to be

---

[7] *Poetry & Prose*, Hayward, op. cit., p. 468.

[8] *Camb. Hist. Eng. Literature*, Vol. IV, 1909; Chap. XI—'Donne' by H. J. C. Grierson.

in turn betrayed and overcome by Donne's passionate love for, and secret marriage with Ann More. Again, we see the prison and hardships he had fled from by his apostasy overtaking him after his marriage, and later when he and Ann were forced to live in poverty and galling dependence at Pyrford, and at Mitcham, in the early years of their married life. Lastly, we note the spiritual side of his nature which he had tried to barter for his ambitions, reasserting itself when, ironically, Donne was forced to earn his living as secretary to Thomas Morton one of King James's favourite chaplains, in the controversy being waged between the Churches, and the final triumph of this spiritual side—of what J. B. Leishman would call Donne's 'Muse of Theology' —when he took orders in the Anglican Church, in January 1615.

It would seem that in the love of Ann and in the care of his large family Donne found a temporary respite from the fretting dualisms of his nature. The sufferings detailed in his letters 'from mine hospital at Mitcham' are all external, having to do with his own passing illnesses or those of his children, or with reverses of fortune. That his love for Ann was constant and deep is proved by many instances, and by references in his letters, as for example, in a letter to Sir Robert More in 1614 explaining why he will not leave her in solitude:

So much company therefore, as I am, she shall not want; and we had not one another at so cheap a rate as that we should ever be weary of one another.[9]

These were the years of his great prose works: *Biathanatos*, *Pseudo-Martyr* and *Ignatius his Conclave* in which the controversial qualities of his intelligence had free play, while the spiritual side of his nature was nourished by his extensive reading in the Fathers and in Scripture. The *Divine Poems* and *Holy Sonnets*, together with the *First Anniversary* and *Second Anniversary*, all composed between 1609 and 1615, lack much of the dramatic and passionate immediacy of the *Songs and Sonets*. Their dialectic is, as it were, at one remove and lacks bite, evidence perhaps that the fierce passions had been tamed, the inner dialectic made quiescent.

The *Holy Sonnet XIX*: 'Oh, to vex me, contraryes meet in one . . .'— one of the three sonnets which Helen Gardner thinks were written

---

[9] Quoted by Mrs. J. Bennett in 'The Love Poetry of J. Donne', *Seventeenth Century Studies presented to Sir H. Grierson*, 1938, p. 89.

after his ordination—is purely an objective cataloguing of the incon-
sistencies Donne has perceived in his own temperament and which he
likens to a 'fantastique Ague'.

> As humorous is my contritione
> As my prophane Love, and as soone forgott:
> As ridlingly distemper'd, cold and hott . . .

> . . . to-day
> In prayers, and flattering speaches I court God:
> To morrow I quake with true feare of his rod . . .

The last line of the Sonnet:

> Those are my best dayes, when I shake with feare.

brings to our minds the image of a more staid Donne looking back,
with perhaps an unconscious nostalgia like that of an old soldier for
the battlefield, to the maelstrom of his earlier years, when arrogance
had fought with fear, dare-devilry with a canny instinct, worldly
ambition with religious beliefs, passion with prudence, flesh with
spirit . . . They were over now—

> the weeping and the laughter
> Love and desire and hate . . .

and the dialectic which will frame the Divine Poems, and especially
the sermons and the devotional works of his mature years, though still
intimate, colloquial and passionate, will lack that sense of living stress,
of tension, which is the glory of his greatest poems.

Man hath weav'd out a net, and this net throwne
Upon the Heavens, and now they are his owne . . .
But keepes the earth her round proportion still? . . .

The First Anniversary

CHAPTER II

THE MACROCOSM

IF DONNE himself can be regarded as a living symbol for the pulsating dialectic of his verse, he can be looked on also as a symbol for the divided world into which he was born. Herbert Read sees Donne's mind 'poised at the exact turn of the course of Philosophy'. It may be truer to say that he is a man torn both ways; curious about and welcoming the new Knowledge, but drawing his inspiration from, and sharing deep affinity with the old.

Students of Donne are very much divided about 'placing' him. Miss Ramsay claims that the whole cast of his thought was medieval.[1] Mr. Moloney, on the other hand, thinks that he rejected the medieval synthesis, though he admits that Donne, more strikingly than either Shakespeare or Milton, is an exemplar of the 'divided mind' of the time.

> 'It was the peculiar tragedy of Donne,' he writes, 'to be born at a time when the medieval synthesis of flesh and spirit had indeed not been entirely forgotten, but when its validity had been seriously challenged.'[2]

Though Courthope,[3] at the other extreme, speaks of Donne as the first of the moderns, both he and Grierson[4] agree on the basic principle that the tortuous metaphysical style peculiar to Donne is the expression of the gradual disintegration of medieval thought, brought about by the upheavals of the times and the new individualism of the Renaissance. This I think is the more correct view.

The classical-Christian 'world structure' in which Donne belonged by intellectual temper and spiritual affinity had been built up over many centuries out of tradition, religion and experience, and was chiefly based on the Aristotelian-Ptolemaic philosophy of the cosmos. In this view, man on earth was at the very heart of the universe: in the great chain of being descending from God through angels and men to animals, and to organic and inorganic matter, he occupied the unique station between the spiritual and the animal order, at once aspirant and

---

[1] M. P. Ramsay, *Les doctrines médiévales chez Donne*, 1924.
[2] M. F. Moloney, *J. Donne: His Flight from Mediaevalism*, 1944, Chaps. III and IV.
[3] W. J. Courthope, *History of English Poetry*, 1903.
[4] H. J. C. Grierson, *Background of English Literature*, 1934, p. 115.

slave; in the physical- and Christian-order, he was lord of the central, stationary planet, the earth, which, surrounded by layers of the other three elements, air, fire and water, belonged in a system of concentric spheres which housed the sun, moon, stars and other planets, all their diverse patterns and opposing forces controlled by an overruling, omniscient divine law; and, finally, in his composite character as a being of mind and body, of spirit and matter, man was the microcosmic parallel to God and the Universe, epitomizing in himself all systems, all creatures, yoking together and reconciling the contradictory elements of the spiritual and the material in that extremely delicate balance, that 'subtle knot' of personality, which captivated the imagination of Donne, and provided him with the impetus to resolve the baffling enigmas of the human situation by seeking analogies in what would seem to the unthinking, the most alien and most unlikely of areas.

This orderly classical-Christian world-view was gradually undermined by the Copernican revolution, aided by the new scientific discoveries of the 17th century. It is said that man's imagination must have been staggered when he learned that, far from being at the hub of a stable universe, he was no more than an inhabitant of one of the smallest of countless worlds whirling about in a new heliocentric dimension. But we must remember that this revolution in man's thinking was not in the nature of a sudden upheaval. Douglas Bush points out that it took well over a century for the new theories to gain full acceptance, even among the learned.[5] It was more in the nature of a gradual unfolding of new knowledge, a progression of discoveries, as with the telescopic observations of Galileo, and the appearance of new stars in 1572 and again in 1604, which contradicted, with no violent shock to the intelligence, former notions of the immutability of super-lunary regions.

Curtis in his history of the English University reminds us that in the 1580s, close to the time when Donne was at Oxford, candidates for the M.A. debated the possibility of a plurality of worlds, giving, from Clark's *Register*, the phrasings of the questions:

> In 1581 'An plures sint aut esse possint mundi?' . . .
> in 1588 'An sint plures mundi?' . . .
> in 1611 'An luna sit habitabilis?'[6]

---

[5] D. Bush, 'Science & Literature': *Seventeenth century Science & the Arts*, ed. H. H. Rhys, 1961.

[6] M. H. Curtis, *Oxford & Cambridge in Transition*, 1959, p. 233, quotation from Andrew Clark, ed., *Register of the University of Oxford*, Vol. II, 1887, pp. 170–177.

That Donne at any rate was not thrown off balance by the new science
can be shown by reference to many passages, both in his intimate
letters to friends, and in his poetic and prose works. Gosse[7] reminds us
that Donne was an enthusiastic student of the new developments, and
points out that *Ignatius His Conclave* of 1611, reveals his up-to-date
study of the writings of Galileo and Kepler, and his grasp of the
principles taught by Copernicus and Tycho Brahe. Yet there is no
evidence of panic in his letter to his friend, Sir Henry Goodyer, in
1609, two years before the publication of this work:

> I often compare not you and me, but the sphear in which your
> resolutions are, and my wheel; both I hope concentrique unto
> God: for methinks the new astronomie is thus appliable well, that
> we which are a little earth, should rather move towards God,
> than that he which is fulfilling, and can come no whither, should
> move towards us. To your life full of variety, nothing is old, nor
> new to mine . . .[8]

Koestler detects in *Ignatius His Conclave* 'the clerical attitude of ironical
indifference towards the new system', illustrating it by Donne's
pungent remark in connection with Kepler—the first astronomer in
Europe—

> who (as he himselfe testifies of himselfe), ever since Tycho Brahe's
> death hath received it into his care, that no new thing should be
> done in heaven without his knowledge.[9]

There is no evidence, either, of undue alarm on Donne's part in his
poem *The First Anniversary*, despite the lines that some critics quote to
prove just the contrary:

> And new Philosophy calls all in doubt . . .
> The sun is lost, and th' earth, and no mans wit
> Can well direct him where to looke for it.

Here we have but a humorous presentation of the contemporary
situation in philosophy and science, which Donne exploits to serve

---

[7] E. Gosse, *Life & Letters of J. Donne*, 1899.

[8] *Poetry & Prose*, Hayward, p. 459.

[9] A. Koestler, *The Sleepwalkers*, 1959, pp. 214, 370.

the purpose of his poem, which is, as the sub-title tells us, to anatomize the present world, to demonstrate its 'frailty and decay', to expose its absurdities and contradictions, and above all, its bewildering flux . . .

> So short a life, that every peasant strives,
> In a torne house, or field, to have three lives . . .
> mankinde decayes so soone,
> We' are scarce our Fathers shadowes cast at noone . . .,

and to contrast all this with the changeless ideal which he saw embodied in Elizabeth Drury's resurrected spirit—

> She that was best, and first originall
> Of all faire copies . . .

and the ostensible subject of the poem.

This is not to say that Donne rejoices in the changes brought about by the new philosophy. There is a pathos in the lines:

> 'Tis all in pieces, all cohaerence gone . . .

which points to his regret that the old familiar order has passed away forever; that the scholastic preoccupation with metaphysical knowledge connected with Being and Essence is being replaced by the concentration of scientists on the evidence of the telescope and the new instruments of measurement; that the age of faith, and hence of wonder, has given way to a restless and soul-destroying scepticism.

To sum up, it is my belief that Donne's steadfast faith, his being 'concentrique unto God', kept him from being overwhelmed by the drastic rearrangement of the universe. In the heart of his being he knew that what mattered ultimately was not whether the world itself was geocentric or heliocentric, but that man should preserve his place in the divine order, that he should be theo-centric.

> I need not call in new Philosophy, that denies a settlednesse . . .
> but makes the Earth to move in that place, where we thought
> the Sunne had moved; I need not that help, that the Earth itselfe
> is in Motion, to prove this, that nothing upon Earth is permanent
> . . .[10]

---

[10] *Poetry & Prose*, Hayward, op. cit., p. 674.

We shall find Donne constantly preoccupied with this theme of permanence and of lasting reality, not merely on the physical plane, but on the more intimate plane of human relationships: man's relationship with his fellow man, particularly in the union of human love where Donne finds a permanence that transcends time; and, finally, man's relationship with his Creator, with Ultimate, unchanging Reality which in the end will be his all-in-all. The lasting effect which the new age made upon Donne was that he became more intensely aware of the values which seemed to be vanishing forever—the old religious unity, the privileged position of man in the ancient hierarchy, the old familiar certainties which the new science called in question—all that in the racial memory had been real and permanent and reliable. It is values and enduring realities such as these, that Donne is ever seeking by means of his vigorous and often ruthless dialectic, both in the turmoil of his own inner experience and in the flux of religious, political and scientific affairs without. We shall find, as we study the *Songs and Sonets*, that many of them are concerned with this theme of making a new unity, a wholeness defying change, a reality that will abide.

DONNE IN RELATION TO THE POETRY OF HIS TIME

Much of the contemporary criticism of Donne's verse is derogatory, the classic example perhaps being found in a letter written to Dr. Arthur Johnston, by William Drummond of Hawthornden, probably between 1625–1630:

> In vain have some men of late (Transformers of everything) con-
> sulted upon her (Poetry's) reformation, and endeavoured to
> abstract her to Metaphysical ideas and Scholastic Quiddities, denud-
> ing her of her own Habits, and those ornaments with which she
> hath amused the whole world some thousand years.[11]

It is interesting to note that Drummond treats the terms 'metaphysical' and 'scholastic' as synonymous. He objects to Donne's innovation as an outrage on the traditional poetic practice which was to embellish and beautify, certainly not to argue in dialectical terms, nor,

> the deeper knowledge of dark truths so teach,
> As sense might judge, what phansie could not reach.[12]

The whole difference between Donne and his contemporaries lies in the contrast offered by these two words of Carew's: 'sense' and 'phansie'; for Donne was boldly original, particularly in his early poems, in using poetry to portray not the ideal but the real, not

> A Mimique fury, when our soules must bee
> Possest, or with Anacreons Extasie,
> Or Pindars, not their owne . . .

but with the intelligent adult's experience of reality in all its intensity and immediacy. Here again it is Donne's innate desire for what is real and permanent which affects not only the language but the very form of his verse. While his great predecessors and contemporaries, for the most part, portray, in true Petrarchan fashion, the ideal lover and beloved in an Arcadian setting, speaking their love in conventional phrases and postures, Donne records the real situation with all its human incon-sistencies, its conflicting emotions of love and hate, and its opposing tones of seriousness and mockery, in vivid colloquial idiom, vibrating

---

[11] *The Works of Drummond of Hawthornden*, 1711, p. 143.
[12] Thomas Carew, '*An Elegie upon the death of Dr. John Donne*', 1633.

with felt passion which is very remote from the stereotyped phrasing of the sonneteers.

No estimate of Donne has ever surpassed that made of him by Thomas Carew in this *Elegie*, written soon after his death, extracts from which have already been quoted. He goes to the heart of Donne's achievements:

> The Muses garden with Pedantique weedes
> O'rspred, was purg'd by thee; The lazie seeds
> Of servile imitation throwne away;
> And fresh invention planted . . .
>
> Thou hast . . . drawne a line
> Of masculine expression . . .
>
> Since to the awe of thy imperious wit
> Our stubborne language bends, made only fit
> With her tough-thick-rib'd hoopes to gird about
> Thy Giant phansie, which had prov'd too stout
> For their soft melting Phrases.

Later on we hope to comment on the 'line of masculine expression'. Here attention is drawn only to some of the *Songs and Sonets* which show a strongly anti-romantic bias. In these Leishman would maintain that Donne was 'cocking snooks at the Petrarchan adoration and Platonic idealism of Spenser and the Sonneteers, flouting conventions which he and many of his contemporaries felt to have lasted too long . . . inspired by that spirit . . . which has so often made young men feel (as Virginia Woolf said of James Joyce) that in order to breathe they must break the windows.'[13]

Take first of all Donne's *Song*: 'Goe, and catche a falling starre . . .' Though certainly some 'windows had been broken' by poets such as Wyatt, Chapman and Sidney, there was not until Donne's time such a wholesale breach of all the sacred rules of decorum. One has but to compare this *Song* with favourite contemporary lyrics, such as Michael Drayton's

> I pray thee, leave, love me no more . . .

or Thomas Campion's

> Follow thy fair sun, unhappy shadow . . .

---

[13] J. B. Leishman, *The Monarch of Wit*, 1951, p. 145.

to estimate the shock Donne must have caused by his grave poetic
gaffe. Here we find the light lyric form forced to bear the harsh, jarring
consonants of 'a mandrake root', and to be almost totally subjected to
a boisterous colloquial diction. Thus, the title and the form of the poem
both belie the cynical content which has its climax in stanza three:

> If thou findst one, let mee know,
> Such a Pilgrimage were sweet;
> Yet doe not, I would not goe,
> Though at next doore wee might meet,
> Though shee were true, when you met her,
> And last, till you write your letter,
>   Yet shee
>   Will bee
> False, ere I come, to two, or three.

—a climax which has been built up, quite logically, from the high-
spirited exaggeration of the preceding stanzas. Of such practice Grierson would remark that Donne in revolting against one convention
was cultivating another: a deliberate cynicism and sensuality which
should be taken no more seriously than the idealizing worship of the
sonneteers. That is true. What Donne's close circle of friends, amongst
whom was Ben Jonson, valued in such poems was their wit. Here the
'tough reasonableness beneath the slight lyric grace' is heightened by
the mock-serious exaggeration and satiric inversion, as for instance in
stanza two where the finding of 'a woman true and fair' is proposed as
a wonder beyond belief. The wit is of course further strengthened and
made more delightful by the typically scrupulous Donnean logic,
which, while piling exaggeration upon exaggeration:

> Tell me, where all past yeares are . . .
> Ride ten thousand daies and nights,
> Till age, snow white haires on thee . . .

still has a subtly persuasive power upon the intellect.

A similar technique is used with more or less success in other poems
such as The Baite, The Blossome, Break of Day, The Indifferent, The
Message, Communitie—where conventional forms, images or attitudes
are deliberately travestied by Donne in his—often—harshly zealous
poetic-apostolate of reality.

The delightful comic ingenuity, the technical skill, the formal logical

devices, the intimate colloquial tone, and especially the witty appropriateness of the parody were all aspects that appealed strongly to the
coterie of men of wit amongst whom Donne circulated these poems
in manuscript, and that caused him to be hailed as the admired origin-
ator of the 'strong line' rather than as a parvenu or iconoclast. But
always deeper than the delightfully witty play of intellect, and masked
by the mockery, was Donne's passion to 'cut out the cant', to have
done with posturing, and to portray experience in its living reality and
human totality.

Like G. K. Chesterton, Donne would contend (I think) that the
only correct view of the contemporary world is that obtained by
standing on one's head. So, in *The Indifferent*, we find him standing
the accepted standards of Petrarchan behaviour and verse on their
heads in his praise of inconstancy, in his reference to faithful lovers as
'poore heritiques in love', and in his outrageous acceptance of vice as
normal. But in the light of the contemporary court and social life of
the London Donne knew so well, we have to admit that his poem,
though exaggerated, is yet closer to real life than the poetic platitudes
about fidelity, so wearily uttered by the swains and their mistresses in
the sonnets.

The Indifferent is a splendid example of Donne's method. We note
the antithetic yet logical pattern of stanza one leading up to the climax
—and the shock—of the final line:

> I can love any, so she be not true;

the deliberate anti-romantic tone in these lines from the same stanza:

> Her whom the country form'd, and whom the town,
> Her who beleeves, and her who tries,
> Her who still weepes with spungie eyes,
> And her who is dry corke, and never cries . . .;

the passionate, disruptive rhythm of stanza two with its ambiguous
terms and suggestive wit, so vividly portraying the disenchanted lover,
all leading up quite logically and in Donne's best mock-serious tone
to the final inversion in stanza three, of the conventional analogy between love and religion:

> . . . alas, Some two or three
> Poore Heretiques in love there bee,
> Which think to stablish dangerous **constancie** . . .

People who find such poems as this 'shocking' are reading them without sufficient understanding either of Donne's poetic intentions, or
of the times for which he wrote. To be shocked is, I think, in most
cases to admit a refusal to accept the realities of our human condition,
to show a strange ignorance of our very make-up.

> If reality revolts us, if we merely turn away from it in disgust, to
> whom shall we sacrifice it? How shall we make of it a gift to God
> and to man?

asks Fr. Thomas Merton in *No Man is an Island*—a title very aptly
borrowed from one of Donne's sermons.

But reality, as Eliot reminded us, is not always an easy thing to bear,
a pleasant thing to face. Evidently Donne thought otherwise and in
some of the *Songs and Sonets*, but more especially in the *Elegies,* his
realism is perhaps too brutal, too reactionary. In his zeal to expose the
fallacies of the typical love sonnets he emphasises the actuality hidden
beneath the platitudinous metaphors. Compare these stereotyped
images from a single poem ('*Rosaline*' by Thomas Lodge):

> Her eyes are sapphires set in snow . . .
> Her cheeks are like the blushing cloud
> Her neck like to a stately tower . . .

with this from Donne:

> Thy head is like a rough-hewne statue of jeat,
> Where marks for eyes, nose, mouth, are yet scarce set.
> > *Elegie VIII*

or with the justly-criticised extravagance of:

> And like a bunch of ragged carrets stand
> The short swolne fingers of thy gouty hand
> > *Elegie VIII*

These, one must admit, are extreme instances of Donne's anti-romantic
method. Still they do help to illustrate the great service he rendered
English poetry, almost singlehanded, rescuing it from the cloying
sweetness, the formal rhetoric, the self-conscious posturing, the worn-
out images, and giving it new life, new meaning, in the intimacy, and

often deliberately shocking directness of his verse. R. Skelton sums up the position:

> without the forthrightness, the passion, the realism of Donne, we might possibly, never have recovered from the 'good taste' of the court poets of his period. Only Ben Jonson can stand beside him as a reformer and an originator of new structures, and it was the combined influence of these two that accounted for a great deal of what is best in the poetry of the following hundred years.[14]

Here then, in Donne's reactions to the contemporary worlds of religion, science, philosophy and poetry into which he was born, we find another example of those contradictions peculiar to his make-up, and from which came naturally the living dialectic of his verse. For we find that while his whole aspiration was towards the security of the old order as represented by the medieval synthesis, he yet was the keen student of the new sciences, as is proved by his treating in his *Essays in Divinity* (1614–15) of such an up-to-date work on the Copernican theory as William Gilbert's *De Magnete* (published in 1600), and by his plentiful references to the new learning in his other works and poems.

In his Christmas Day Sermon, 1621, Donne makes the remark:

> Knowledge cannot save us, but we cannot be saved without Knowledge; Faith is not on this side Knowledge, but beyond it; we must necessarily come to Knowledge first, though we must not stay at it . . .[15]

And in another sermon preached in December 1626 he remarks:

> . . . if there be any addition to Knowledge, it is rather a new Knowledge, than a greater Knowledge . . .[16]

In the realm of religion we have already seen the contradiction in his own life between his lineage and his conduct: Donne the descendant of St. Thomas More, heir to a noble Catholic tradition forsaking that cause, and, seemingly, bartering his birthright for worldly gain. Then again we have the contradictions of the harsh and arrogant satirist,

---

[14] Robin Skelton, 'Elizabethan Poetry', *Stratford-upon-Avon Studies 2*, 1960.
[15] *Poetry & Prose*, Hayward, op. cit., p. 709.
[16] Ibid., p. 672.

playing the part of obsequious servant of the great in so many of his personal and his verse-letters to his patrons, both of the poetic and the courtly circles. And finally, we have Donne the poet, on whose shelves must have been the works of Spenser and Sidney as well as collections of contemporary verse (some written by his uncles) in such anthologies as *The Paradyse of Daynty Devises*, who while working in traditional forms, using traditional subjects, yet became one of the most boldly original of all English poets in his handling of poetic practices and language.

There does appear to have been in Donne, to a greater extent than in most men, a mixture of coward and rebel. It was out of the inevitable conflict between these two sides of his nature, out of this 'womb of war', to quote Dylan Thomas, and this living dialectic, that Donne made his greatest poetry. He lacked the aristocrat's balance of temperament, the knightly soul of Sidney, the urbane detached manner of Ben Jonson or Marvell. Intensely aware of the dichotomy within himself he sought—as we shall see more clearly in Chapter IV—the balance of the 'via media', the security of the Aristotelian 'mean', to give permanence and stability to his life; while his fear of and hatred for extremes, coupled with his hatred for the unreal, made him rebel alike against man-made penal laws and the poetic conventions of his day.

Because he was too honest to escape the reality of the struggle within himself in romantic dreams, or to put consistency before the truth, his poems possess the tension and ambiguity which belong to the complexity of a living experience, and it is these qualities which give a permanent value to his work.

'The history of a curriculum may be dull in comparison with the detailing of events in the forum, or in the field, but these events, from the middle ages on, are largely shaped by men who have themselves been formed in the microcosm of the University.'

W. T. Costello: *The Scholastic Curriculum*, p. 2.

CHAPTER III

THE MICROCOSM OF THE UNIVERSITY

OF DONNE'S early education we have no certain details. It is likely, as Walton asserts, that he had the benefit of a private tutor up to his tenth year, and it can be assumed, I think, that this tutor would have been a Jesuit. It is doubtful, however, whether it is entirely reasonable to conclude, as does Professor Martz, that Donne was 'subjected to a strong Jesuit influence during his formative years', and that this influence should affect, in the fundamental way Martz suggests, the very form and content of his poetry.[1]

We do know with certainty from official University records that John Donne and his brother, Henry, were entered in 1584 at Hart Hall, Oxford, which, under its great principal, Philip Rondell (1549-'99), had become the 'refuge for the adherents of the old religion'.[2] Here Donne remained for three years, following the normal course of studies for an Arts Degree, for which he did not however qualify since, as a Catholic, he could not subscribe to the required oath. Walton declares that from Oxford Donne went on to Cambridge, but this fact is not authenticated in any of the official documents of that University.

There can be no doubt that the period spent by Donne at Oxford had a very strong formative influence on the development of his personality. Free at last from the unnatural restraint and the crippling fear of his childhood, which we can infer from his own admission already quoted on page 8:

> I had my first breeding and conversation with men of a suppressed and afflicted religion, accustomed to the despite of death, and hungry of an imagined martyrdome,

we can presume that in the calm of academic Oxford and its age-old scholastic discipline, his rich gifts of mind and heart developed rapidly. All our mature attitudes—our entire approach to reality, in fact, as Basil Willey reminds us—depend upon our predispositions, and these in turn depend to a large extent upon our training. It is intended

---

[1] L. L. Martz, *The Poetry of Meditation*, 1954, p. 38.

[2] C. E. Mallet, *History of the University of Oxford*, 1924, Vol. II, p. 297.

in this chapter to examine in what Donne's training in Oxford consisted, to study the details of the curriculum and the routine of the academic programme which he followed, in order to find out to what degree it whetted—or satisfied—his admitted 'hydroptique immoderate desire of humane learning'[3], and so to try to estimate its influence on his later poetic practices.

---

[3] Letter to Sir H. Goodyer, 1608, *Poetry & Prose*, Hayward, p. 456.

THE SCHOLASTIC CURRICULUM IN SIXTEENTH CENTURY OXFORD

The curriculum at Oxford at the end of the sixteenth century when Donne studied there, and well on into the seventeenth century, was still, in the main, the old scholastic curriculum with its emphasis on the teaching of dialectic and the works of Aristotle, its history and tradition reaching back to the old Carolingian schools of the eighth century, and to the greater schools and Abbeys of the thirteenth century, and proud to name among its exponents Alcuin and Maurus, St. Thomas Aquinas and Peter Abelard.

> 'The first thing to note about the curriculum', remarks Curtis, 'is its traditional character. The structure of the liberal arts had been set in the period of the late Roman Empire . . . the arts course at Elizabethan Oxford and Cambridge shows its derivation from this pattern . . .'[4]

That Alcuin was a living name even in Donne's time is proved by the printing in two editions in the sixteenth century, and three editions in the seventeenth century, of his *De Dialectica*, the first logic textbook written by an Englishman, containing the basic principles of Aristotle's logic as understood by commentators on the *Organon*.[5]

In his history of the university of Cambridge, Mullinger[6] points out that logic began to acquire a place of real interest in English education as a result of the establishment at Oxford and Cambridge, in the twelfth century, of the seven liberal arts from which the scholastic programme developed. The principal works on logic compiled between the twelfth and sixteenth century were all based on Aristotle's *Organon*, the list of authors including such names as John of Salisbury, Alexander of Hales, Vincent of Beauvais. Early in the sixteenth century the didactic allegory of Stephen Hawes, *The Pastime of Pleasure*, set out to teach the true value of logic: 'to devyde the good and the evyl a sondre', and to propose a course of training in the seven liberal arts as the proper preparation for the good life. Several of the textbooks used by the university students in those years were written by their lecturers in the course of their work. In 1545, the *Dialectica* of John Seton, fellow and lecturer at St. John's College, Cambridge, first appeared in print, and despite his adherence to the old religion, it was reissued in 1560, in

---

[4] M. H. Curtis, *Oxford & Cambridge in Transition 1558-1642*, 1959, p. 86.
[5] See W. S. Howell, *Logic & Rhetoric in England 1500-1700*, 1956.
[6] J. B. Mullinger, *The University of Cambridge*, p. 342.

1572, and again and again before the end of the century.[7] The *Dialectica* is regarded by scholars as the last work of importance in the history of scholastic logic in England. Together with *The Rule of Reason, containing the arte of logique, set forth in Englishe*, by Thomas Wilson, published in 1557, it was regarded as the standard textbook for students at the Universities.

Historians such as Sir C. E. Mallet[8] and S. E. Morison,[9] as well as critics and authors like C. M. Coffin[10] and Hardin Craig[11] insist on the special dialectical and Aristotelian characteristics of the sixteenth century University curriculum. Fr. Costello's study of the scholastic curriculum,[12] though concerned mainly with seventeenth century Cambridge, is very valuable because of the light it throws upon the times from an unusual and little-studied angle. His sources were, in his own words, 'the miscellaneous contents of the seventeenth century student's wastebasket'—note-books and thesis broadsides—through a critical and interpretative résumé of which he allows us a glimpse into the student mind as it was being shaped at the University. That Fr. Costello's material is relevant to our study of the curriculum at Oxford, is confirmed by a remark from a contemporary, Nicholas Fitzherbert, to the effect that Oxford

> so resembles Cambridge in the method of instruction that the two Universities may reasonably be rivals.[13]

Fr. Costello also stresses the dialectical and Aristotelian nature of the curriculum and depicts the typical student as forever expounding, defining, distinguishing and disputing.

At Oxford, in 1584 when Donne was entered there, the programme of studies was still in the main dictated by the Statutes of Edward VI as revised by Queen Elizabeth in 1564—towards an even greater conservatism. Under the Edwardian Statutes the course of studies leading

---

[7] M. H. Curtis, op. cit., p. 106, and Note F, p. 284.

[8] C. E. Mallet, *History of the University of Oxford*, 1924, Vol. II.

[9] S. E. Morison, *The Founding of Harvard College*, 1930.

[10] C. M. Coffin, *John Donne & the New Philosophy*, 1937.

[11] H. Craig, *The Enchanted Glass*, 1952.

[12] W. T. Costello, *The Scholastic Curriculum at early 17th century Cambridge*, 1958.

[13] N. Fitzherbert, *Oxoniensis Academiae Descriptio*, 1602, quoted by Costello on p. 2.

to B.A. was arranged thus: first year—mathematics; second year—dialectic; third year—philosophy. It may be remarked here that the terms 'logic' and 'dialectic' were interchangeable at all medieval and Renaissance universities. From the details which Fr. Costello gives us of the changes brought about in the Cambridge curriculum by the Queen, in the decrees of 1559 and 1571, we can assume that her revision at Oxford followed on similar lines. To give greater emphasis to the study of dialectic, it was decreed that the programme for B.A. should follow a new pattern: first year—rhetoric; second and third year—dialectic; fourth year—philosophy.

Both Craig and Curtis attribute this new focus on dialectic to the advent of Protestantism, to an age when the

> whole subject of religion was debated by larger parts of the population than had ever debated any subject before, and when men in public life were successful in proportion to their polemical skill . . .[14]

Though Curtis is more interested in the increased content and status provided for the arts course by putting rhetoric and grammar on a par with logic, he admits that

> logic still occupied a major role in a liberal education, that academic achievement continued to be measured by disputations, and that the authority of Aristotle, here as elsewhere, maintained high prestige.[15]

In Donne's time then it is well established that the two great arts of communication, rhetoric and logic (or dialectic), were given considerable prominence in the university curriculum at Oxford. It is interesting to note that in many of the logical and rhetorical treatises of this period, the metaphor of the closed fist representing logic, and of the open hand, the symbol for rhetoric (which was borrowed from Zeno through Cicero and Quintilian) is used to explain the preoccupation of logic with the tight discourses of the philosopher and the dialectician, and that of rhetoric with the more open discourses of

---

[14] *The Enchanted Glass*, op. cit., Chap. VI.
[15] *Oxford & Cambridge in Transition*, op. cit., p. 96.

the orator.[16] At the end of his first year, having mastered the 'figures' and 'colours' of rhetoric, the student could then give his entire attention to the study of logic and dialectic—

> the divine mistress, logic, which deriving its name from intellect and reason (in the Greek), guides this highest operation of man and directs it against error . . .[17]

---

[16] In his *Devotions upon Emergent Occasions* (1623), Donne refers to this figure: 'The art of proving, logique, and the art of perswading, Rhetorique, are deduced to the hand, and that expressed by a hand contracted into a fist, and this by a hand enlarged and expanded.' *Poetry & Prose*, Hayward, op. cit., p. 545.

[17] From 17th century student's notebook in B.M., quoted by Fr. Costello in *The Scholastic Curriculum*, op. cit.

The Aristotelian Character of the Curriculum

It is the agreed opinion of scholars, describing the tradition in English scholasticism of the sixteenth century, that the logical treatises of Aristotle, as construed by commentators of his own pagan world and by their Christian and Mohammedan followers, were the ruling authorities. Fr. Costello claims that the study of Aristotle at Cambridge, emphasized in the reforms of Henry VIII in 1535, was confirmed by Queen Elizabeth in 1570, and that Aristotelianism, i.e., Aristotle's ideas of substance, accident, potency, soul, matter and form, made by St. Thomas into a Christian philosophic system with a theory of ontology and of knowledge in the new Aristotelian terms, this 'basic Aristotelianism' Fr. Costello demonstrates 'had become, and was still, the heart of the scholastic method and doctrine at the beginning of the seventeenth century.'[18] Curtis would maintain that this was judging the curriculum strictly by the Statutes which took no account of the extra-statutory forces, for example the new interest in science and geography at Oxford, and in Ramism, chiefly at Cambridge, which, little by little were to undermine men's faith in the old order. But the old order still stood firm; and Curtis agrees with Mallet, despite his censuring him for his deprecation of change in that nebulous extra-statutory realm of University life, that time and again in various statutes between 1583 and the early years of the seventeenth century, the authority of Aristotle was vindicated afresh, both in the method and in the matter of the College programmes. As late as 1636, the Laudian statutes of Oxford required that candidates for degrees should argue their propositions in logic, rhetoric, politics and moral philosophy, according to the teachings of Aristotle, 'whose authority is paramount'.[19]

Finally, we have Morison's well substantiated claim[20] that during the first five centuries of University history, Aristotle, 'the master of them that know', wielded an authority such as no one intellect had exerted before or since; that he provided the student of those centuries with both method and matter—a logical organon for reaching the truth and a corpus of secular knowledge in practically every subject except law and medicine; and that, lastly, the Aristotelian classification of knowledge long outlasted the revolution wrought by the new

---

[18] W. T. Costello, *The Scholastic Curriculum*, op. cit., p. 169.
[19] M. H. Curtis, *Oxford & Cambridge in Transition*, op. cit., p. 229.
[20] S. E. Morison, *Founding of Harvard College*, op. cit., Section on Medieval Universities.

scientific methods, and was little, if at all disturbed, by the new Ramist logicians of the Reformation.

It may be opportune to consider here the controversy in connection with Peter Ramus (1515–72), the French humanist made famous by his revolt against Aristotelianism, and to try to estimate the extent of his influence, if any, on John Donne, and on the dialectical method employed in his poetry. Ever since Hardin Craig,[21] P. Miller,[22] and in particular Rosemond Tuve[23] took up his cause, claiming for him what seems an exaggerated rôle in the penetration of literature by logic during the late sixteenth and early seventeenth centuries, critics and historians have questioned the validity of their theses—some roundly refuting them. Thus we have Professor Nelson speaking of the 'distortion' in their estimate of Ramus whom he dubs 'a clever ignoramus'[24]; G. Watson, who, though critical of Nelson's method of attack, yet is at one with him in condemning the 'pretensions made for the literary influence of Ramus by Professors Hardin Craig, Percy Miller and Rosemond Tuve', and considers Professor Tuve's work an' essentially unliterary pursuit'[25]; W. Empson, who thinks that Miss Tuve, like Dryden, failed to see the point in Donne's subtle handling of imagery[26]; Professor McLuhan, who, denying any Ramistic influence on Donne, claims that his style is based on his study of the Fathers of the Church, and reminds us that Donne was known to his contemporaries as 'our English Tertullian'[27]; and finally, we have A. J. Smith who sees the high claims put forward for Ramus in the field of poetry, by Miss Tuve, as a distortion not worthy of serious attention.[28]

It is a pity that Professor Tuve's admirable study of the logical qualities in the metaphysical image, generally, and of its employment in poetry, should be vitiated by what I consider her one-sided view of the history of logic itself, and of its connection with English literature

---

[21] The Enchanted Glass, 1952.

[22] The New English Mind: the 17th century, 1939.

[23] Elizabethan & Metaphysical Imagery, 1947.

[24] Univ. of Michigan Contributions in Mod. Philology, No. 2, April 1947, N. E. Nelson 'Peter Ramus & the confusion of logic, rhetoric & poetry'.

[25] Mod. Philology, Vol. LV, No. 4, May 1958, G. Watson: 'Ramus, Tuve & the New Petromachia'.

[26] W. Empson, Kenyon Review, Autumn 1949, 'Donne & the Rhetorical Tradition'.

[27] H. M. McLuhan, Hudson Review, Vol. I, No. 2, 1948, 'Tradition & the Academic Talent'.

[28] A. J. Smith, RES, Vol. VII, No. 28, Oct. 1956, 'Examination of Claims for Ramism'.

in the sixteenth and early seventeenth centuries. Her tracing of the
logical function of the image; her marking for us the preciseness with
which Donne chooses metaphors which will predicate truly; her
emphasis on what is one of the outstanding characteristics of his verse—
his examination and setting out of 'the true nature of a subject, with
axioms in the form of images that go to make their mark like bullets'[29];
and her relating of all this to the logical training Donne and other
metaphysical poets received during their formal education: all this is
excellently done. But that the qualities of those poems which are regarded as metaphysical, including the 'grand dialectical pursuit of
distinguishing the true from the false'[30]; or the conception of an
infinite number of logical relationships in a divinely ordered universe;
or the poet's pursuit by dialectical means of these arguments or relationships which would lead him to a knowledge of reality[31]—that these
qualities should be attributed, in toto, to the influence of a parvenu in
the centuries-old tradition of Aristotelian or scholastic logic, is a claim
which cannot, I think, be reasonably accepted.

The naïvety of such remarks as these:

> The Ramist adduces his examples to prove not that poetry is
> logically complicated, but that logic is natural to poets, as to all
> reasoning men;[32]

and Miss Tuve's defying of

> even the twentieth century reader . . . to come away from a
> Ramist handbook still able to keep poetry and logic in separate
> compartments[33]

is exposed by the simple historical and literary fact that the concern
of Ramism with poetry was purely utilitarian, employing it to illustrate various definitions and methods in logic. Ramus's aim from the
beginning was to reform teaching, not to revolutionize poetry. His
achievement should be judged within the realm in which it applied,
not distorted or exaggerated to force a false hypothesis.

While it is true that in Ch. XII Miss Tuve admits that Ramus

---

[29] R. Tuve, *Elizabethan & Metaphysical Imagery*, op. cit., Chap. XII, p. 343.
[30] Ibid., Chap. XII, p. 337.
[31] Ibid., p. 346.
[32] Ibid., p. 338.
[33] Ibid., p. 335.

constituted an 'added influence' in the traditional field of peripatetic logic, one cannot help feeling that, on the whole, her judgment is less than fair to the great names in the academic history of the Universities—Aristotle and St. Thomas Aquinas in particular—when she commits herself to such a statement as this, concerning Donne:

> I do not think it possible to read through the major contentions in any Ramist handbook, and follow this with a re-reading of Donne's poems, without arriving at the notion that these intellectual developments of Donne's day *explain his processes of thought,* and his own attitudes towards such processes, far more satisfactorily than any of the current popular phrases about 'feeling his thought'.[34] (The italics are mine.)

I am convinced that Donne's early training in logic and dialectic was a major factor in developing his mode of thinking, his habit of expression, his penchant for endless analysis, his argumentative bent, but I do not think that this is by any means the whole story. Other factors must be considered—and yet in the end one must admit that no listing of influences, no study of curricula, no examination of his methods, no dissection of his imagery, will ever fully 'explain his processes of thought', or unravel the mystery of the poet, lover and dialectician which is Donne.

It is interesting to note how contemporary views on Ramism seem to stress its utilitarian character—sometimes in a slightly mocking tone as if suggesting that this new fashion in logic was not to be taken too seriously.

Professor Watson's quotations from two contemporary Cambridge plays are a fair indication of Ramus's prestige among the playwrights:

> For tidy Peter like a pretty primmer
> May well be learned ere thou go to dinner.
>
>   from *Tyros Roring Magge*;

and:

> Mr. Peter maketh all things very plaine and easie
>   from *Three Parnassus Plays,* 1598–1601.[35]

---

[34] R. Tuve, op. cit., p. 351.
[35] G. Watson, *Modern Philology,* Vol. LV, No. 4, May 1958.

Craig would agree with these remarks, for he hails Ramus as

the greatest master of the short-cut the world has ever known.[36]

But that such simplified methods could have appealed to the keen intellect of Donne, who loved to sweep the deeps of learning and to climb the tortuous mazes of the mind, is not I think, in the nature of things, possible.

More contemporary evidence is to be found in the verse-preface to Carter's annotations of Seton's *Dialectica*, published soon after the first Ramist Dialectic was printed in London, in 1574. Here, Thomas Drant appends the name of Ramus to his catalogue of logicians in some telling lines, which play upon the latin meaning of ramus (branch):

Yet helpful is Ramus, as if he alone were the fruit-bearer,
Thrusts he forth grape-clusters joyful, with Phoebus smiling the while.
The force of examples adorns him as do . . . also finitenesse and use . . .[37]

Later, in 1593, Richard Hooker after a lavish praising of Aristotle in his work *Of the Laws of Ecclesiasticall Politie*, has this to say of 'Ramystry':

(it is) an art which teacheth the way of speedie discourse, and restrayneth the minde of man that it may not waxe over-wise.[38]

And John Case, writing about the controversy between the old ways and the new, in his *Speculum Moralium Quaestionum*, the earliest book printed at the newly set-up Oxford press in 1585, thinks that the young choose Ramus because

the young exalt such apostasy . . . I do not blame Ramus in this, for he was learned; I rather exalt Aristotle, for he stands out above all.[39]

---

[36] *The Enchanted Glass*, op. cit., Chap. VI.
[37] W. S. Howell, *Logic & Rhetoric in England*, op. cit., Chap. II.
[38] Quoted by W. S. Howell, ibid.
[39] Quoted by J. B. Mullinger in *The Univ. of Cambridge*, op. cit., II, p. 411, Note I, trans. by W. S. Howell.

What then is the true position of Ramus in the history of University education in the sixteenth century? Fr. W. J. Ong's scholarly work, *Method, Ramus and the Decay of Dialogue*,[40] together with his study of *Ramus, and the Transit to the Modern Mind*,[41] give one of the fairest accounts of the history and influence of Ramism. The fame of Peter Ramus began with the publication of his thesis in 1536:

Everything that Aristotle taught is false.

It is a remarkable fact that after such an audacious beginning none of his later works, not even his mature *Lectures on Dialectic*, is concerned with any positive or original thesis, but rather with commentaries on the works of Aristotle's *Organon*. His stated aim was:

to put the logical books of the *Organon* to the service of erudition,[42]

i.e., to be the great popularizer of Aristotle by applying the rules of logic to the material of life, particularly to poetry. His works are therefore—to use Fr. Ong's phrase—'larded with excerpts' from the great Latin poets and orators, in accordance with the Ramist principle, that any kind of discourse, provided it was well done, was as good an example of logic or dialectic as any other. Far from serving the development of poetry of any kind, Ramism made poetry its servant in the pursuit of its own pedagogical ends. That is what earned for Ramus the nickname of 'usuarius':[43] a kind of purveyor of logic, a man well qualified to edit, had circumstances offered, a 'Logic Without Tears'. While supporting Miss Tuve's contention that Ramus strengthened the position and prestige of logic in the hierarchy of learning, Curtis believes that he did so by considerably simplifying the traditional organization of the subject, emphasising the process rather than the formal abstract rules for making arguments.

Adamson contends that Ramus contributed really nothing to the history of logic, and that his theories 'acquired for a brief period a fictitious importance from their connection with the general revolt

---

[40] W. J. Ong, *Method, Ramus & the Decay of Dialogue*, Harvard Univ. Press, 1958.

[41] W. J. Ong, 'Ramus—Transit to Mod. Mind', *Mod. Scholasticism*, XXXI, 1955.

[42] *Method, Ramus & Decay of Dialogue*, op. cit., p. 41.

[43] F. P. Graves, *P. Ramus & the Educational Reformation of the 16th C.*, 1912, p. 57.

against Aristotelianism, and with the Protestant struggle against the Roman Catholic authority.[44]

This balanced view agrees, in the main, with what Curtis has to say of the influence of Ramism in Oxford and Cambridge. Ramism was introduced into the English Universities, in the early days and to an inconsiderable degree, through Ascham,[45] and later, more purposefully, through the humanists—Gabriel Harvey, Professor of Rhetoric at Cambridge from 1574, and John Rainolds, the Puritan President of Corpus Christi College, Oxford.[46] Curtis maintains that this introduction of Ramism into the English Colleges represents the beginning of the challenge to traditional intellectual dogma and authority. In an interesting note he tells us that in Rainold's copy of Aristotle's *De Arte dicendi libri tres*, preserved in the Bodleian Library, there is a neatly written interleaved commentary, in which the views of Ramus are frequently cited and contrasted with those of Aristotle.

'The attitudes of Rainolds and Harvey', he remarks, 'strongly reflected the self-conscious and anti-authoritarian approach of Peter Ramus'.[47]

But the point to bear in mind is that during Donne's term at Oxford and well into the seventeenth century, Aristotle was the master on whose work the commentaries continued to be written, around whom the controversies raged and the extra-statutory studies were centred.

Although histories of logic agree that Cambridge alone became the stronghold of Ramism in England, Fr. Ong has no hesitation in declaring that

in so far as logic was maintained at the University level in England, it tended to remain pretty much Aristotle.[48]

And both Graves and Mallet claim that at Oxford Ramism made no headway; and that late in the sixteenth century statutes were still being promulgated ordering bachelors and undergraduates

---

[44] R. Adamson, *Short History of Logic*, 1911, p. 168.

[45] L. P. Ryan, *Roger Ascham*, 1963, pp. 148, 269.

[46] *Oxford & Cambridge in Transition*, op. cit., pp. 119 and 197.

[47] Ibid., p. 252.

[48] W. J. Ong, *Method, Ramus & the Decay of Dialogue*, op. cit., p. 304.

to lay aside contentious authors and to follow only Aristotle and those that defended him.[49]

The Rules drawn up by James Duport, fellow of Trinity College, Cambridge, from 1627, repeat this injunction:

> Follow not Ramus in logic nor Lipsius in Latin, but Aristotle in one and Tully in the other.[50]

To stress the over-riding influence of Ramus in the fields of either logic or poetry, is to focus one's attention on a mere offshoot—or a mere branch, if one may risk the pun—and to neglect the great tree whose roots run deep and far into the medieval and scholastic past. One does not need the testimony of a Walton—who tells us that at his death Donne left

> the resultance of 1400 Authors, most of them abridged and analysed with his own hand[51]

to prove that it was the giants of the past that shaped his mind. The evidence is in his own works, not only in the many direct references and quotations, but in the numerous conceits whose wit is based on Aristotelian and scholastic concepts and doctrines. Apart altogether from the evidence offered in this Chapter for the Aristotelian nature of the sixteenth century Oxford curriculum, one would be surprised if Donne with his hunger to know the essences of things, and their ultimate sources and values, were satisfied with 'short-cuts' and 'digests' when he could go to the great fountain-heads of knowledge themselves.

---

[49] C. E. Mallet, *Hist. of the Univ. of Oxford*, op. cit., p. 147.
[50] Quoted by Curtis in *Oxford & Cambridge in Transition*, op. cit., p. 116.
[51] *Walton's Lives*, 1903, 'Life of Donne', p. 63.

The Dialectical Character of the Curriculum

While, strictly speaking, logic is the art of thinking correctly, and dialectic, according to Aristotle is

> that part of the art of discoursing which provides us with the arguments with which we can dispute either side of a question with a certain probability,[52]

both terms were used interchangeably at Renaissance Universities and for long afterwards. I think that Fr. Gilby puts the distinction very well:

> 'Logic,' he remarks, 'is like Ariel, lacking the touch of feeling, needing to be kindled by dialectic at play in the world of sensibility, probability and motion, and differing from rhetoric, not because it is cold, but because instead of an audience it has a friendly opponent.'[53]

Because of the numerous critics who blame the University course in logic for filling the world with 'logic-choppers', I should like to look at some contemporary, i.e. sixteenth century views on the subject, which should act as a corrective. At the beginning of Thomas Wilson's *The Rule of Reason*, published in 1557, we find a little verse praising the seven liberal arts and including

> Logique by art settes forth the truth,
> And doth tel us what is vayne . . .[54]

Fr. Costello quotes from a typical seventeenth century student notebook, now in Cambridge University Library, this definition:

> Logic's concern is to speak the truth . . . define what is obscure, divide what is universal, and reason to the truth among verisimilars.

All the notebooks examined by Fr. Costello are agreed upon this point: that the object of logic is the attaining of truth. There were of course then, as now, the numerous 'nugiloqui ventilatores' as John of

[52] W. J. Ong, *Method, Ramus & Decay of Dialogue*, op. cit., p. 216.
[53] T. Gilby, *Barbara Celarent*, 1949, p. 35.
[54] W. S. Howell, *Logic & Rhetoric in England*, op. cit., Chap. II.

Salisbury styled them: the 'fans of futile phrases', but, as Fr. Gilby so justly points out (on p. 11),

> if they were accused of logic-chopping, we shall be more accurate if we mean that they chopped with, not at, logic.

Lastly, Lord Herbert of Cherbury in his Autobiography, while condemning the wranglers at the Universities, adds:

> I approve those parts of logic which teach men to deduce their proofs from firm and undoubted principles, and show men to distinguish betwixt truth and falsehood, and help them to discover fallacies, sophisms . . . and vicious argumentations . . .[55]

The truth which the student sought by the study of logic and dialectic was the truth about the whole of reality—man and the universe—as revealed in the Christianized cosmology of Aristotle: a universe in which all matter was seen to be made up of attributes, divided into ten different Categories, governed by a Divine order manifesting itself in a vast spiral of correspondences, with man himself holding the key position between angel and beast, a microcosm, reflecting on the physical and material side, in detail, the great pattern of the macrocosm, and on the spiritual side, the image of God Himself, though dimmed by the Fall. It was this logical view of the universe through the 'prisms of the Aristotelian predicables and predicaments' that imparted to Donne his conviction that he was 'a little world made cunningly', and that taught him to use logical analogy as an instrument for the discovery of reality. Here in the traditional idea about correspondences we find the root of his obsession with the metaphysical image of the microcosm, which Craig rightly sees as an attempt to grasp an aspect of unity.

Professor Tuve demonstrates[56] that these ten Categories, or Predicaments, are the real springs of imagery for the metaphysical poets, using illustrations from Donne's poem, A Jeat Ring Sent:

> Thou art not so blacke, as my heart,
> Nor halfe so brittle, as her heart, art thou;
> What would'st thou say? shall both our properties by thee bee spoke,
> Nothing more endlesse, nothing sooner broke?

---

[55] Quoted by W. T. Costello in The Scholastic Curriculum, op. cit., p. 48.
[56] R. Tuve, Elizabethan & Metaphysical Imagery, op. cit., Chap. XI.

Here Donne is examining, through the various categories, the real nature of the fragile jet ring, so as to demonstrate by means of its properties and accidents, in a wittily fallacious manner, corresponding qualities in his and his mistress's hearts. The poem is logical and convincing certainly, but its chief merit and attraction lie in its wit. This is the point which Miss Tuve seems to miss in her insistence on the Ramist influence, because, as Bethell points out in his brilliant essay on the conceit of the argument:

> If this is taken Ramistically, it is not wit but science; it remains wit only while its foundation is Aristotle and its process dialectically fallacious.[57]

The wit in many other poems, as we shall see later, depends upon Donne's ingenuity in detecting the logical relationships, and in making imaginative connections between the different realms of being. This is often carried out by him in a mock-serious manner, as in *Loves Progress*, where the properties and accidents of gold are investigated, and then paralleled with the qualities of womankind, in order to justify man's use of both. *The Second Anniversary*, as well as the hyperbolic *Verse Letter to the Countesse of Huntingdon*, play upon the logical difference between substance (or essence) and accident:

> Though you a wifes and mothers name retaine,
> 'Tis not a woman, for all are not soe,
> But vertue having made you vertue, 'is faine
> T'adhere in these names, her and you to show . . .
>
> *The Verse Letter*

and in the *Second Anniversary*, we have Donne's advice to

> Study, are thou fall
> On accidentall joyes, th' essentiall . . .
> The sight of God in fulnesse . . .

We must remember that thinking in logical fashion was natural to Donne. It was never mere dilettantism. Without the training in formal logic he would no doubt have reasoned keenly and brilliantly; with it the tool of his thinking was sharpened making him into the subtle

---

[57] S. L. Bethell, *Gracian, Tesauro & the Nature of Metaphysical Wit*, 1953.

metaphysical poet who loved to analyse the very basis of reality from the Categories of Being.

In Chap. IV we shall see how Donne's many far-fetched images have, for the most part, logical bases. If they seemed abstruse and difficult to his later readers, we must remember that they were not so to his contemporaries to whom logic had given the tools for thinking.

'So deeply had the language of logic entered into the English vocabulary by Shakespeare's time', comments H. Craig, 'that usually one cannot tell whether Shakespeare is aware of the logical denotations, or connotations either, of his language or the forms of his thought'.[58]

Besides a study of the categories, the predicables and the causes, by means of which he sought to penetrate and grasp reality, the University student had also to master the various arguments in logic based on Aristotle's *Prior Analytics*, to learn to proceed from proposition to proposition in an effort to arrive at the truth by means of reason. One of the seventeenth century students' notebooks quoted by Fr. Costello, gives this definition of the argument: 'Res rationem dubiae rei fidem faciens'—the method of arriving at the probable, or of resolving the uncertain.

Of these arguments the chief was the syllogism (together with its compressed form, the enthymeme) which by a process of deduction and induction led to a probable conclusion. The intricacy and subtlety of the rules connected with the syllogism, together with its various kinds, forms and fallacies, must certainly have taxed the mental powers of the seventeenth century student. Syllogisms in all forms abound in Donne's poems, for serious as well as for sophisticated purposes, and in many cases as in *The Prohibition* for example, they determine the structure of the poem. The more interesting poems are those based on Donne's witty use of the syllogism. *The Will*, which Mr. Leishman calls an 'astonishing example of prodigious wit', owes both its shape and its tone to the inverted form of the syllogism. Here Donne ruefully examines the illogicality experienced in his love, and applies it to the dispositions which he ordains in his will. Instead of the usual order of major and minor premise followed by a logical conclusion or deduction, Donne astounds us in the opening line with the ready-made and paradoxical decision of his will. Then he goes on, like the good debater

---

[58] H. Craig, *The Enchanted Glass*, 1952, Chap. VI.

he is, to convince us by the logical 'deus ex machina' of his major premise. Thus, he leaves his money to a Capuchin, because love has taught him

> Onely to give to such as have an incapacitie.

The wit is compressed, startling and all-pervading, yet constant to Donne's logical pattern:

> Here I bequeath
> Mine eyes to Argus, if mine eyes can see,
> If they be blinde, then Love, I give them thee,
> My tongue to Fame; to 'Embassadours mine eares . . .
> Thou, Love, hast taught mee heretofore
> By making mee serve her who had twenty more,
> That I should give to none, but such, as had too much before.

It is remarkable with what ease Donne can change from this tone of banter to one of gentle seriousness, without in any way injuring the consistency of the poem:

> I give my reputation to those
> Which were my friends; Mine industrie to foes;
> To Schoolemen I bequeath my doubtfulnesse; . . .
> To Nature, all that I in Ryme have writ;
> And to my company my wit.
> Thou, Love, by making me adore
> Her, who begot this love in me before,
> Taughtst me to make, as though I gave, when I did but restore.

Because the object of the logicians was to seek truth, the student was trained early in his course to recognize the many fallacies he might meet in argument. Fr. Costello notes that in a seventeenth century notebook preserved in Queen's College, Cambridge, there are thirteen fallacies listed under two headings: fallacies of speech and fallacies of things in themselves. He remarks, pertinently, that such an emphasis on the detection of logical fallacies should prove that the Renaissance training in logic was not merely a training in quibbling, as is so often maintained.[59] Donne, as we shall see later, put his knowledge of

---

[59] *The Scholastic Curriculum*, op. cit., p. 54.

the fallacies to witty use in many of his poems. In the *Communitie* and *The Flea* for example, he uses them not to trick us by sophistry but very often to highlight a greater truth which we might otherwise miss. Bethell argues eloquently that

> all wit in the form of argument is deliberately fallacious, and so presented as to state a truth by implication,[60]

instancing many poems of Donne which will be discussed later.

Leishman thinks that this kind of wit might more appropriately be called 'scholastic' than 'metaphysical', and it is his opinion that Donne's originality consists largely in the fact that he combined this wit with

> the rigidly logical and systematic method of the academic or theological disputation.[61]

Our study of the Oxford disputations will prove the truth of this assertion.

---

[60] *Gracian, Tesauro, & the nature of Metaphysical Wit*, op. cit.,
[61] *The Monarch of Wit*, 1951, p. 81.

The Academic Disputation

The exercise at which the student's grasp of the laws of logic and his ability to detect the various fallacies were tested was the scholastic disputation—a strictly stylized and technical exercise which developed from the dialectical character of the scholastic curriculum, and remained a standard University exercise down to the late seventeenth century. Little changed since medieval times its subject was generally one of the several arts, and comprised an oral discussion, without notes, of some thesis (or proposition) by the recognized rules of logic.

According to Andrew Clark disputations were held at Oxford on the Mondays, Wednesdays and Fridays of every week, from one o'clock to three in the afternoon, at which the moderator made a speech 'in favour of Aristotle and true logic'.[62] For the University requirements each student had to take part in a disputation four times during his years as undergraduate, twice as Respondent (or proposer) and twice as Opponent (or objector). Fr. Costello, illustrating from a complete Cambridge disputation held late in the reign of Queen Elizabeth (now in manuscript in the B.M.), points to the highly technical quality of the various parts. A complete disputation had three separate stages. The Respondent opened with his thesis, for the presentation of which he was allowed half an hour. Then came the answers of his Opponents following a line of syllogisms specially plotted to trap the Respondent into denying his thesis. The final summing-up was done by the presiding Moderator. These exercises were of incalculable value in developing clear-headed, logical methods of thinking, in cultivating a clear-cut, incisive style, in sharpening the wits of the participants, in teaching a delicate care in the use of words, and in the building up of a water-tight argument. Here, in the logical thrusts and parries of the tense Answerer and the wily Opponent lies the heart not only of the disputation itself, but of medieval and Renaissance University life.

There was a definite ritual about the disputations—called 'quadragesimals'—which formed part of the final exercises for the B.A. Beginning on Ash Wednesday with a formal 'sermo ad clerum' and Assembly in the Schools, they continued right through Lent to Holy Week. Each candidate had to 'stare in quadragesima', i.e. to present himself daily,

---

[62] A. Clark, *Register of the Univ. of Oxford*, 1887, II, quoted by Coffin, *John Donne and the New Philosophy*, 1937, p. 32.

from one of the clock until 5 . . . during all which time the com-
mencers are there to be ready to defend 2 or 3 theses, which they
themselves shall make choice of, and deliver unto those Bachelors
of Arts, not of the same College, who shall think fit to come
thither to reply unto them.[63]

At both Oxford and Cambridge these final disputations were, in
general, public demonstrations of the proficiency of a scholar.

Coffin quotes for us some of the subjects of disputations held at
Oxford during the sixteenth century:

An luna sit causa fluxus et refluxus?
Multitudo librorum est studiorum impedimentum,

and Campion's famous disputation:

An inferiora regantur a superioribus?[64]

which attracted the special attention of the Queen during her progress
to Oxford in 1566.

Mallet records that when in 1586 the authority of Aristotle was
vindicated afresh, the regulations regarding the Lenten disputations
were reorganized and re-enforced, and that again and again, down to
1607, subsequent decrees and statutes rehearsed the old academic ritual
for the disputations in parvisis, so very little changed since the days of
Abelard.[65] Early in the seventeenth century, James Duport, Fellow of
Trinity College, Cambridge, drew up . . .

Rules to be observed by Young Pupils and Schollers in the
University . . . When you dispute, think it not enough barely to
pronounce and propound your arguments, but press them, and
then urge them home, and call upon your adversary for an
answer, and leave him not till you have one . . . dispute always
syllogistically, at least enthymematically, and as much as you can,
categorically . . .[66]

---

[63] G. Peacock, *Observations upon the Statutes . . . of Cambridge*, 1841, quoted by
Costello, op. cit., p. 15.

[64] *John Donne & The New Philosophy*, op. cit., p. 31.

[65] C. E. Mallet, *History of Univ. of Oxford*, op. cit., pp. 119; 127–8; 147–148.

[66] Quoted by M. H. Curtis, *Oxford & Cambridge in Transition*, op. cit., p. 113.

It is interesting to note that the disputation was the highlight of official academic entertainment. To see Oxford, Mallet remarks, it was necessary to hear the men of Oxford dispute. During her visits there in 1566 and 1592, the Queen stayed at Christ Church, and was entertained on both occasions by disputations at St. Mary's. On three successive days she heard

> latin philosophical debates Respondents, Determiners and Opponents, all gallantly playing their parts . . . The fact that almost all the hours spent by the Queen outside the gates of Christ Church were occupied, not in visits to the Colleges, but in disputations at St. Mary's, is significant of the part still played by these debates in academic life.[67]

A peculiar character at the Oxford disputations, and one which must have appealed to the puckish wit of Donne, was the 'Terrae Filius'—the official jester—whose function it was to play verbally upon the question under dispute, 'to rail upon the point' as it were, and often of course to lampoon the faculty. Fr. Costello maintains that such Terraefilial disputations continued at Oxford down to 1763, and, moreover, that the Gravediggers' scene in Hamlet is an expert literary adaptation of the performance of a scholastic Terraefilius. Quite often in both the *Songs and Sonets* and in the *Satyres*, one can hear an echo of this old waggish character. In *The Curse*, for instance, the force of the mounting maledictions in the final stanza, reaching a climax in the heavy deliberation of the line:

> Fall on that man . . .

is suddenly exploded by the pert wit of the afterthought:

> The venom of all stepdames, gamsters gall,
> What Tyrans, and their subjects interwish,
> What Plants, Myne, Beasts, Foule, Fish,
> Can contribute, all ill which all
> Prophets, or Poets spake; And all which shall
> Be annex'd in schedules unto this by mee,
> Fall on that man; For if it be a shee
> Nature beforehand hath out-cursed mee.

---

[67] C. E. Mallet, op. cit., pp. 112, 113.

And in *The Sunne Rising*, while we are engaged with the problem of how Donne is going to perform the remarkable feat of eclipsing the sun's powerful beams with a mere wink, our logical house of cards is brought toppling down with the impish reversal in the reasoning:

> But that I would not lose her sight so long . . .

It is my belief that this University background, this intense training in logic and in dialectical disputation had a very strong influence on the youthful Donne, appealing to his keen intelligence, his rare perceptive powers which sought the essence in all things, his lightning wit, while at the same time strengthening the dualistic tendency of his nature. In very many of his poems one can hear distinct echoes from the scholastic debates, with Donne fulfilling at once both the rôles of Respondent and Opponent, recognizing with the clarity of an Augustine or a Paul, the war that continually raged within, between the spirit and the flesh, the will and the appetites of the body.

Thus in *The Canonization* Donne plays the part of a skilful and cunning debater, bold in attack:

> For Godsake hold your tongue and let me love;

deft in manoeuvre:

> Who saies my teares have overflow'd his ground?;

wily in conceding:

> Call us what you will, we are made so by love . . . ,

only to emerge triumphant at the end, turning seeming defeat: 'We can dye by it, if not live by love' into the transcendant victory of the lovers 'canoniz'd for love'.

Again, in *Lovers Infinitenesse*, we hear him dispute lawyer-like, his rights to the 'all' of his mistress's love, examining each counter claim with admirable restraint and a pungent wit, only in the end to sweep all arguments aside with the characteristically disarming surprise of his reversal:

> Yet I would not have all yet,
> Hee that hath all can have no more . . .

a reversal worthy of an intellect honest enough to recognize its own limitations, for to reason by paradox, as Donne so often does both here and elsewhere, is, as Ronald Berman remarks in his *Life of Henry King*, 'to be aware of the impotence of reason itself'.

Another good example of Donne in the old disputatious mood is *Womans Constancy*. We note the disconcerting quality of the opening:

> Now thou hast lov'd me one whole day . . .

which yet carries the implicit accusation of inconstancy; the conscientious sifting of the woman's trumped-up excuses to the nadir of accusation in:

> Or, your owne end to Justifie,
> For having purpos'd change, and falsehood; you
> Can have no way but falsehood to be true;

and then the trump-card of the arch-disputer which by the equivocal tone of its masculine brag seems to belie the boast of his argument:

> Vaine lunatique against these scapes I could
> Dispute, and conquer, if I would,
> Which I abstaine to doe,
> For by to-morrow, I may thinke so too.

Legouis, commenting on another poem, *Loves Deitie*, says he finds it more ingenious than convincing, and adds that the cleverness with which Donne manages to fit all the logical joints might make one contend that he is 'more of a schoolman than a poet when he delights in symmetrical constructions, even to the making of blind windows.'[68] Here we are up against the old condemnation of the scholastic as a mere logic-chopper and quibbler, but it would show a very poor appreciation of Donne's intelligence and wit to try to place him in this category. Legouis does not do so; he refutes this contention in fact, by showing that in several of the *Songs and Sonets* the logic is subordinated to the dramatic element which he values above all. The Schoolman in Donne is never made to type; rather is he forged anew in every poem, on the anvil of his toughly-brilliant intellect, through the passion that hammers through the dialectic of his verse.

---

[68] P. Legouis, *Donne The Craftsman*, 1928, p. 47.

'Hell is the home of the unreal . . .
It is the only refuge from heaven which is . . .
the home of the masters of reality,
and from earth, which is the home of the slaves of reality.'

G. B. Shaw: *Man and Superman*

CHAPTER IV

THE DIALECTIC OF REALITY

THE HUMAN person reaches out to reality by different ways: by means of the senses and the intellect; by way of the imagination and vision; and since the middle ages—especially since the seventeenth century—by means of science. To be the real men and women that God made us—to be truly whole—we need all these ways and means. To be whole is to be perfectly conscious of oneself, to be aware of and to accept one's relationship to the environment, one's place and orientation in the flux of things. It is when one accepts fully that one is really whole. It is interesting to note, by the way, that the words 'holy' and 'whole' have the same etymological root. Fr. Thomas Merton in *No Man is an Island* makes the significant remark that 'everything that is, is beautiful, in so far as it is real', while Fr. Gerald Vann warns us that

> reality is not a nettle to be grasped, or a fruit to be plucked and eaten, but a bride to be wooed . . .[1]

This wholeness, this oneness with reality, is something to which all men aspire from the depths of the diversities and the dichotomies of their natures. Donne, as we have already seen, felt more keenly than most men the near-Manichean cleavage within himself, and it was this consciousness of his dualistic nature which conditioned his 'wooing' of reality, turning it into the truculence of his dialectic, and the merciless probe of his logic.

Paradoxically, it was because of Donne's deeply spiritual nature, because as Teilhard de Chardin would say, 'he preadhered to God', that his attraction to the real was so great. Instinctively he felt the truth of the doctrine that 'God reveals Himself everywhere, beneath our groping efforts, as a universal milieu, only because He is the ultimate point upon which all realities converge . . . Our minds are incapable of grasping a reality, our hearts and hands of seizing the essentially desirable in it, without our being compelled by the very structure of things to go back to the first source of its perfection . . . It is precisely because

---

[1] G. Vann, *The Heart of Man*, 1943, p. 14.

5

God is the centre that He fills the whole sphere . . .'[2] Donne would have been in full agreement with Claudel's remarks on the object of poetry—

> L'objet de la poésie, ce n'est donc pas, comme on le dit souvent, les rêves, les illusions ou les idées. C'est cette *saint réalité*, donnée une fois pour toutes, au centre de laquelle nous sommes placés . . .[3]

Donne did not take the whole of creation for his province; in fact his poetry triumphs by virtue of its limitations. The reality he explored was that most intimately known to himself: his own 'naked, thinking heart' which loved to be 'subtile to plague' itself; his own reactions, in all their complex immediacy—first of all to the realities of human love where Donne found fulfilment and wholeness for a time, and then to that ultimate reality which he found only in God. In all this, Donne was proving himself a true metaphysician because, as Father Kubertanz, S.J., tells us in his *Introduction to the Philosophy of Being*, the proper business of metaphysics is 'the demonstrative knowledge of the real, inasmuch as it is real'.

Another qualification modifies the reality which is the subject of Donne's poetry: he is intensely aware of the fallen nature of the reality of our world; that it was man in perfect concord with reality who fell into the isolation and the duality which we have inherited, and of which he was so conscious. One could say that the wholeness he sought throughout his life was the perfection and harmony of the paradisal state—first, as we have seen, in the experience of human love, and at the end in God Himself—

> th' Eternall root of true love . . .
>
> From: *A Hymne to Christ*

In Donne one sees more clearly than in most men the twofold goal of life: towards individual independence and fulfilment on the one hand, and towards a sense of oneness with reality i.e. people and things outside one's consciousness, on the other. The arrogant rebel whom Gosse first set before our view, and whom so many of the later critics helped to build up, was but a mask to hide the true Donne: the lonely, frightened child, self-revealed in his confession in the Preface to *Biathanatos*; the young student debarred from taking his degree; the

---

[2] Teilhard de Chardin, *Le Milieu Divin*, Fontana Books 1964, p. 114.
[3] Paul Claudel, *Positions et Propositions*, 1928, p. 165.

gay gallant at Cadiz who yet could be no courtier; the earnest lawyer at Lincoln's Inn who could set no sanctions for his own wayward heart. All his life, all he really yearned for was the security of a lasting reality the 'one little room' of his *Good Morrow*. Even in his fiercest satires and most anti-romantic elegies, there is not so much evidence of the rebel flaunting the sacred rules and genres of poetry, as of the insistent dialectician searching, arguing with himself and others, relentlessly sifting the chaff of everyday experience to get to the reality beneath.

The realism of the *Satyres*, and of some of his *Verse Letters*, reveals the bold, independent mind of Donne, the steely appraising eye, which if trained predominantly on the inward scene, missed no detail that passed without. These *Satyres* are full of the savagery of youthful scorn for the false fashions of London society in the 1590s—for the fawning sycophant darting from one 'many-coloured peacock' to

a Captaine . . . Bright parcell gilt, with forty dead mens pay;

for the glib lawyers whom Donne cleverly mocks in the very legal terms that they prostitute; for the gossiping, flattering courtier, who

. . . wiser than all us,
. . . Knowes what ladie is not painted . . .
. . . Knowes who loves; whom; and who by poyson
Hasts to an offices reversion.
                                        Sat. IIII;

for the bribed and corrupt judges whom he mocks in a clever pun:

Judges are Gods; he who made and said them so,
Meant not that men should be forc'd to them to goe,
By meanes of Angels . . .
                                        Sat. V

Drummond reported of Ben Jonson that he esteemed John Donne the first poet in the world in some things, adding:

his verses of the Lost Chaine he hath by heart, and that passage of the Calme, That dust and feathers doe not stirr, all was so quiet . . .[4]

---

[4] *Conversations with Drummond of Hawthornden*, ed. R. F. Patterson, 1923, p. 11

The passage so much admired by Jonson was a couplet from *The Calme*, the verse-letter addressed to Christopher Brooke, describing in realistic and witty detail the calm which succeeded the heavy storm during the Island voyages of 1597:

> No use of lanthornes; and in one place lay
> Feathers and dust, to-day and yesterday . . .

Donne certainly was the first major poet to introduce a salutary realism into English verse. Thomas Carew knew his worth and praised him for purging the Muse's garden of

> the lazie seeds
> Of servile imitation . . .

and adds, that from the 'rifled fields', and

> . . . from those bare lands
> Of what is purely thine, thy only hands
> (And that thy smallest worke) have gleaned more
> Than all those times, and tongues could reape before.
> from his 'Elegie' on Donne.

Critics have observed that the strong sense of the dignity of man which was so marked in Renaissance literature is missing from the work of Donne, and that instead we get a 'pervasive irreverence', a levity in dealing with themes which to other poets were sacred. I think this criticism will disappear when we understand the ironic focus which Donne trained upon the contemporary scene, and the wry humour with which he plied the scalpel of his dialectic . . . 'that questioned the distempered part', cutting away the overgrowth of Petrarchan clichés and laying bare the clean healthy bones, the honest sinews of reality. In this connection I should like to quote a remark made by Yeats in 1912, after reading Grierson's new edition of Donne's poems:

> I notice that the more precise and learned the thought, the greater the beauty, the passion; the intricacies and subtleties of his imagination are the length and depth of the furrow made by his passion. His pedantry and his obscenity—the rock and loam of his Eden—but made me the more certain that one who is but a man like us all, has seen God.[5]

---

[5] *The Letters of W. B. Yeats*, ed. Allan Wade, p. 570.

To some ears this may sound extravagant, but it adds weight to the point I wish to make: that Donne's hunger for reality was, in the final analysis, his hunger for God Himself. With the fine probe of his dialectic he pierced beneath the shams and the poses alike of society and its literature, to reveal the true beauty, the 'sainte réalité' of God's world, the divine milieu in which

> all the elements of the universe touch each other by that which is most inward and ultimate in them . . . the same reality being found in their innermost being—like sunlight in the fragments of a broken mirror—one beneath its multiplicity, unattainable beneath its proximity, and spiritual beneath its materiality.[6]

---

[6] Teilhard de Chardin in *Le Milieu Divin*, op. cit., p. 114.

DISPARATE EXPERIENCE AND NEW WHOLES

In his essay on the Metaphysical Poets—written in 1921— T. S. Eliot has pointed to the difference between the mind of an ordinary man and that of a poet. While the ordinary man's experience is chaotic and fragmentary, the poet's mind he remarks is 'constantly amalgamating disparate experience'—such as falling in love, reading Spinoza, listening to the noise of a typewriter, or attending sensibly to any other stimuli. In the mind of the poet, Eliot affirms, 'these experiences are always forming new wholes.'[7] This does not appear to me a very accurate description of the workings of Donne's mind and I consider Eliot's later estimate of the poet much more to the point:

> His fidelity to emotion as he finds it; his recognition of the complexity of feeling and its rapid alterations and antitheses ... When, therefore, we find a poet who neither suppresses nor falsifies, and who expresses complicated states of mind, we give him welcome ...[8]

Nowadays, with our greater knowledge of psychology, we realize what a disorderly house we keep within, where the rise and fall of our emotions in turn determine and are determined by the flow of consciousness, stimulated by the contact of our minds and senses with the sharp edges of reality all round us. In Donne we recognize a poet, not specially equipped to amalgamate disparate experiences into a new whole, but to portray in poetic form the living flux within, in all its unresolved inconsistencies. In other words, we realize that he is being intellectually honest about his reactions, his feelings and his thoughts. The great attraction of his poetry lies in the fact that in some ways it is an elemental thing—

> Amid whose swift half-intermitted burst
> Huge fragments vaulted like rebounding hail ...

the very hurtle and heave of his thoughts and emotions erupting in the swiftly-flowing lava of his verse, owing whatever wholeness or form it possesses to the controlling power of his passionate dialectic.

---

[7] *Selected Prose*, ed. J. Hayward, 1953; 'The Metaphysical Poets', p. 117.

[8] Quoted by A. Alvarez in *The School of Donne*, 1961, Intro., p. 13, from: 'John Donne', *The Nation and Athenaeum*, xxxiii, 1923, pp. 331–2.

The Canonization is a fine example of Donne's method of portraying within the confines of verse a bewildering complexity of attitudes. Whatever unity the poem can boast comes from the adaptation of a paradox, daringly and wittily transported from divine to human love, and then logically worked out in the figures and arguments of the final verses. If we examine the poem in detail we seem to see Donne in the very vortex of his passionate thoughts, whirled hither and thither, now in vehement argument against the practical side of his nature, again in cynical self-mockery of the romantic, other-worldly part, and at the end attempting to transcend both sides by his conception of his love as an eternal universal 'patterne'.

Hunt remarks that the early stanzas are merely a debater's opening manoeuvre—

> a tactical device for disarming the opposition by recognizing and defining the opponent's point of view, and by seeming to concede to its reasonableness only to make more dramatic the counterturn to the destruction of that position in the reply.[9]

That may well be true, particularly in the case of such a wily dialectician as John Donne, but the point to remember is that his opponent here is none other than his own practical commonsense. What wonderfully comes across from this poem is the living argument, the volcano in action, which was Donne himself. The ambiguity of tone is marvellously sustained, and enforced at the end when one would have expected the poem to come to rest in a quiet resolution.

> You . . .
> Who did the whole worlds soule contract, and drove
> Into the glasses of your eyes . . .
> Countries, Townes, Courts: Beg from above
> A patterne of your love!

The vehemence of stanza one springs from the quality of its highly condensed thought expressed through the successive 'jets' of phrases. The 'might-have-beens': wealth, a place at Court, rank, are all juxtaposed with the stark reality of his 'ruin'd fortune', and the pathetic personal details of his gout and the 'five gray haires'. The final line of the stanza—

> So you will let me love

---

[9] C. Hunt, *Donne's Poetry*, 1954, p. 75.

seems to give assurance, for the time being, that Donne has no regrets, that the world, in his case, was indeed well lost for love.

As the poem progresses this assurance begins to flag. In stanza two we find Donne appraising himself with wry amusement as indeed the very embodiment of the standard Petrarchan lover.

> What merchants ships have my sighs drown'd?
> Who saies my teares have overflow'd his ground? . . .

The irony continues into stanza three, but the mockery gradually gives way to serious reflection which is evident in the choice of conventional metaphors and their sublimation into the altogether serious analogy of the Phoenix; and this, combining as it does the qualities of both birds and taper, presents in one dazzling metaphor the very essence of the love which Donne celebrates:

> . . . we two being one, are it . . .

> We dye and rise the same, and prove
> Mysterious by this love.

Here we have a new assertion, that though social outcasts, dead to the world, the lovers possess the power of rising, phoenix-like, to a new life which transcends the mere practical life of reason and of sense. This assertion grows stronger in the next stanza:

> Wee can dye by it, if not live by love . . .

and suddenly justifies itself by its bold equation of the lovers with religious martyrs, both of whom can be said to 'die to the world' for love of a higher good. There is here, however, no final resolution of the problem, and one can perhaps detect a 'sour-grapes' inflection in Donne's lines:

> As well a well wrought urne becomes
> The greatest ashes, as halfe-acre tombes . . .

The emotional and intellectual climax of the lovers being 'canoniz'd for love' is defined in the last stanza, where the image of the martyr gives place to that of the hermit:

> You whom reverend love
> Made one anothers hermitage . . .

The ambiguity of tone which gives the poem its value derives from Donne's ability to present all sides of an argument with honesty and forcefulness. The disparate experiences and moods are here exposed to our full view. However strongly Donne has put the case for the spirituality and other-worldliness of the lovers, we know that he is too honest not to concede the justice of the practical arguments which oppose and mock it. The act of ascetic renunciation is, after all, a long way from the lover whose hermitage is another's body, and in whom he hopes to find epitomized the other worldly pleasures he has foregone.

What we have charted in this poem is the rise and fall of Donne's thoughts and emotions, what Pascal would call 'la peinture de la pensée'. And this seems to me a more fitting description of Donne's method than T. S. Eliot's 'new whole' or his later summary:

> . . . there is in Donne's poetry hardly any attempt at organization; rather a puzzled and humorous shuffling of the pieces.[10]

Yeats shows Donne's influence when in his *Autobiographies* he explains how he tried to write out of his emotions 'exactly as they came to me in life', and to that end employed colloquial and dramatic elements in order that 'the hearer would feel the presence of a man thinking and feeling.'

The rich complexity, the unresolved tensions in Donne's poems, are not due to some psychological quirk, nor to the schizophrenic nature of his temperament. The ambiguity to which they give rise is due finally to Donne's honest appraisal of all that impinges on his life, and especially to his impartiality when he sits as judge at the bar of his own conscience. He accepts the fact that life is complex, and the mind and heart of man almost infinitely so.

The creation of a technique—chiefly the dialectic method, and its tool, the metaphysical image—which would reflect the moving flux of the subconscious, and the subtleties of the human heart, is probably Donne's greatest contribution to English poetry.

---

[10] *A Garland for John Donne*, ed. T. Spencer, Harvard Univ. Press, 1931, p. 8: 'Donne in our Time' by T. S. Eliot.

'THE APPLIED METAPHYSICS OF POETRY':
THE METAPHYSICAL IMAGE

Dr. Johnson did a disservice to the metaphysical poets in drawing attention to the strange tools they used in their poetic exploration of reality rather than to the 'worlds on worlds', and the worlds within worlds, which their poems open up for us. It is unfortunate that his discriminating praise of the poets is sometimes lost sight of:

> . . . if they frequently threw away their wit upon false conceits, they likewise sometimes struck out unexpected truth: if their conceits were far-fetched, they were often worth the carriage . . .

while his definition of their wit remains for too many the distinguishing mark of metaphysical poetry:

> a kind of 'discordia concors'; a combination of dissimilar images, or discovery of occult resemblances in things apparently unlike . . . The most heterogeneous ideas are yoked by violence together . . .

His chief criticism of these seventeenth century poets was directed towards the extravagance of their style and method which he saw as

> a voluntary deviation from nature in pursuit of something strange and new.[11]

W. P. Ker would not agree with this method of judging metaphysical imagery. He would test it by its sensitivity, by its appropriateness in serving the purpose of the poet. I know no better evaluation of Donne's images than his:

> 'Their charm lies' he says 'in the spirit that informs them; his far-fetched images are precious for the sake of the high adventurous spirit that wandered out in such strange seas of thought in search of them.'[12]

---

[11] S. Johnson, *Lives of the English Poets*, ed. G. Birkbeck Hill, 1896, Vol. I, pp. 19–21; 35.

[12] W. P. Ker, *On Modern Literature*, 1956, p. 214.

But for Donne they were not, after all, such strange seas of thought, nor did he ever deviate from nature merely for the sake of novelty, as Dr. Johnson asserts. We have to remind ourselves that Donne's view of the world was the Classical-Christian view in which all creatures, all things, all ideas were linked together by analogy and correspondence. To him it was quite natural to yoke together apparently unrelated things; they were not, in fact, unrelated. It was his keen wit, trained on this world picture, which pierced beneath appearances to discover the underlying reality, and it was to these strange explorations that Donne brought the metaphysical tool of the image, in an attempt to grasp and lay bare, yet hold together in an intellectually satisfying vision, a 'bursting universe'. 'Metaphor', remarks B. Ifor-Evans in *English Literature*, 'is the applied metaphysics of poetry'. Through it Donne sought to bring order into complexity by finding connections between the hierarchies of being, and especially between the microcosm and the macrocosm; by its means he searched for the metaphysical unity which would give meaning to the heterogeneity and the imbalance he experienced within and without himself; above all, he used it as an instrument to explore the fringes of consciousness and the frontiers of the spirit, where the spiritual and the material meet, as G. K. Chesterton so wonderfully says, in a sort of marriage. The conceit, the paradox and the pun, with their linking of different realms of being and of thought, are at once the result of Donne's vision of the poetic of correspondences in all things, and the instrument for his analysis and exploration of reality.

I should like to examine here, briefly, Donne's technique in a poem in which the choice of image has been much criticised.

A Valediction: Forbidding Mourning

In a threefold movement, suggestive of the syllogism, and of the very order of thought itself, Donne sets out to prove his thesis: that the quality of true love, being spiritual, can suffer no change or division, and hence precludes mourning when the lovers are physically parted.

First, we have the proposition stated, and supported by two analogies:

> Our parting must cause as little fuss as do the deaths of 'virtuous men', and they must be as unspectacular as the—supposed— 'trepidation of the spheares'.

In the second movement we have the argument developing to support the proposition, which is again illustrated by two analogies. Note the syllogistic arrangement of this argument:

> A love which depends upon the senses cannot bear bodily absence.
> But our love does not depend upon the senses;
> Therefore it can endure physical absence . . .
> 'Care lesse, eyes, lips, and hands to misse'.

When two such souls are parted they endure not

> '. . . a breach, but an expansion,
> Like gold to ayery thinnesse beate'.

And then we have expressed as a concession in the second analogy, the famous compass image:

> If they be two, they are two so
> As stiffe twin compasses are two . . .

W. P. Ker remarks that it is the critics who make much of this image, not Donne . . .

> who describes the lovers' parting not in the language of geometry but of souls:[13]

> Thy soule the fixt foot, makes no show
> To move, but doth, if the other doe . . .

Donne's logical and dramatic powers fuse in the choice of phrases which while predicating truly of the image, dramatize in a significant and moving manner the essence of the relationship apprehended by him—in this case, the mutual trusting love between himself and his wife:

> And though it in the center sit,
> Yet when the other far doth rome,
> It leanes, and hearkens after it,
> And growes erect, as that comes home.

---

[13] *On Modern Literature*, p. 214.

In 'leanes' and 'hearkens' we have not alone the image, but the very gesture of the waiting, loving wife.

The resolution in the final movement is still perfectly in keeping with the cool logic of the poem, and still employs the image of the compass to say some of the sublimest things ever addressed by lover to his beloved:

> Such wilt thou be to mee, who must
> Like th' other foot, obliquely runne;
> Thy firmnes drawes my circle just,
> And makes me end, where I begunne.

It is the constancy of his wife's love, her 'firmnes', which will help him steer a straight course past the beckoning byways of life, and in the end draw his wandering heart home to its centre and its rest in her.

Concerning this image, Dr. Johnson had once said:

> . . . it may be doubted whether absurdity or ingenuity has the better claim.[14]

But, in this poem, which we know was written for his wife on the eve of his departure for France with Sir Robert Drury, Donne was being neither absurd nor ingenious. If, as Coleridge asserts, images

> become proofs of original genius only in so far as they are modified by a predominant passion,[15]

then this image of Donne's is a proof both of his genius and his passion. The symbol of the compass does not tell us what his love is like, but it does tell us what it is, in terms as precise as those from the Categories in the scholastic textbooks. We must not forget, however, that here as elsewhere in the poems of Donne, the image is subordinate to the dialectic which it serves to illustrate, and that both owe their compelling power to the passionate intellect which forged them.

The images in *The Will* and in *The Relique* are alike in the way that the shock, which their seeming incongruity offers to our sensibility, is followed by a deeper realization of their significance, with our recognition of their logical appositeness.

---

[14] *Lives of the English Poets*, 1896, Vol. I, p. 28.
[15] *Biographia Literaria*, ed. G. Watson, 1956, Chap. XV, p. 177.

> . . . All your graces no more use shall have
> Than a Sun dyall in a grave.
>
> from The Will

Here Donne is saying: just as the function of the sun-dial to record
the progress of the light- and life-giving sun is frustrated by the confines of the grave, so your graces will be robbed of their radiance, and
of their power to enrich forever this fleeting moment of time, if they
are denied their natural function in love.

The much-quoted image from *The Relique* is even more startling:

> When my grave is broke up againe . . .
> And he that digs it, spies
> A bracelet of bright haire about the bone . . .

In both poems Donne is doing much the same thing: the juxtaposition
of a shining brightness with the darkness of the grave, and of graceful
beauty with its empty sterility, heighten the positive values of the
power of beauty and of love which Donne wishes to emphasize in
these poems.

A brief examination of a few more of Donne's images will be an
indication to us of ideas which were important to him, ideas related
to his ceaseless search for the ultimate reality in the centre of the human
vortex, and to his desire to present that reality in all its nuances of
meaning and of feeling.

An important recurring image in poems celebrating perfect love,
e.g., *A Valediction: forbidding Mourning, The Good-Morrow, The Sunne
Rising,* is that of the sphere or circle, or of the two hemispheres which
together make one perfect sphere. The circle, as symbol of something
perfect and eternal, Donne owes to Aristotle, and we find very frequent
mention of it in his sermons:

> One of the most convenient Hieroglyphicks of God, is a circle.[16]

Another image, which might be called the supreme metaphysical
image since it defines relationships in the realm of being, is that of the
microcosm or the macrocosm. It is by means of this image that the
lover's grief at parting from the beloved in *A Valediction: Of Weeping*,
is heightened and given cosmic affinities. Since it is she who has made

---

[16] L. P. Smith, *Donne's Sermons*, 1919, p. 134.

his world, he declares, she should forbear to destroy it—and him—by her weeping.

> On a round ball
> A workeman that hath copies by, can lay
> An Europe, Afrique, and an Asia,
> And quickly make that, which was nothing, All,
>   So doth each teare,
>   Which thee doth weare,
> A globe, yea world by that impression grow . . .

Here, as in the *Valediction: forbidding Mourning*, the truth of the logic and the steady progression of the argument help to deepen the feeling, while the various images employed: his tears, which become coins of great worth because bearing her stamp—'pregnant of thee'—a variant of the popular Elizabethan idea of 'making babies with the eyes'— yet too, the forerunners of disaster, because

> 'When a teare falls, that thou falls which it bore . . .';

and his loved one's tears which become the sea and the tempest threatening his heaven—these images are the tools of the dialectic, teasing the thought, as it were, and giving the measure of the passion which shaped them.

In *The Nocturnall*, which will be studied in detail later, this image is again employed. Here the death of the world becomes almost the 'objective correlative' for the poet's own spiritual disintegration at the death of the loved one:

> The worlds whole sap is sunke . . .

Other images used by Donne demonstrate clearly the function he intended them to fulfil in his dialectical examination of reality. His awareness of the properties and accidents in their component terms is remarkable in this connection, and points to the analytic mind always searching for the foundations, the essences of things. We have seen for example in *A Jeat Ring Sent*, that the wit of the entire poem depends upon Donne's logical investigation of the image. In *Loves Progress*, where Donne seeks to justify the healthy actuality of human love, the argument turns on the difference between properties and accidents—between the true essence and what are merely adjuncts:

> I, when I value gold, may think upon
> The ductilness, the application . . .
> From rust, from soil, from fire ever free:
> But if I love it, 'tis because 'tis made
> By our new nature (Use) the soul of trade.

Thence to the neat application and the clenching of his argument:

> Can men more injure women than to say
> They love them for that, by which they're not they?
> . . . virtue is not she:
> As beauty' is not nor wealth: He that strayes thus
> From her to hers, is more adulterous,
> Then if he took her maid.

This is pure Donne: the logical acumen, the broken rhythm suggesting the dramatic argument, and particularly the witty sophistry of classing and judging human virtue as a mere adjunct, on equal terms with the ductileness and other properties of gold, and in so doing, satirizing the society in which such judgments are made—all these are of the very essence of the poet who is a realist and an intellectual before all else.

THE PARADOX

In his use of the paradox Donne was perhaps influenced more by the writings of the Fathers of the Church, in which wit in the form of paradox played so great a part, than by the Italian poets of the Cinquecento, e.g., Tasso and Berni, to whose 'capitoli' Sidney refers in his *Apologie*. Fr. Ong rightly relates the literary paradox to the superparadox at the heart of the Christian economy, where the tension springs from a maximum of certitude combined with a minimum of understanding.[17] The 'father-mother' paradox found in Donne's Holy Sonnet: *La Corona*—addressed to Our Lady—

---

[17] W. J. Ong, 'Wit and Mystery', *Speculum—Journal of Medieval Studies*—XXII, No. 3, 1947.

... thou art now
Thy Makers maker, and thy Fathers mother ...

can be traced from St. Augustine's sermon:

Denique natus est Christus et de patre et de matre; et sine patre
et sine matre; de patre Deus, de matre homo; sine matre Deus,
sine patre homo ... ,

and from a twelfth century sequence of Adam of St. Victor:

Verbum patris sine matre
Facta mater sine patre
Genuit in tempore.

In the same way, the theology of the Word has proved an inexhaustible
source of conceits down through the ages from the early Fathers,
through St. Thomas Aquinas and the medieval theologians, to seventeenth century poets and divines, down to T. S. Eliot's *Gerontian*:

The Word within a word unable to speak a word ...

It is my belief that the paradox as used by Donne is based on the old
Socratic idea which he found in the Fathers, in whom he had read so
deeply. The aim of the Socratic paradox was to bring into violent
collision the world of appearance and the world of reality, in order
to show the radical incoherence of the one when juxtaposed with the
ultimate coherence and self-evidence of the world of realities. This is
certainly Donne's aim in many of his poems, e.g., *Loves Progress*, to
which I have just referred, and Elegie X: *The Dreame*, in which the
dialectic operates between fantasy and reality:

So, if I dreame I have you, I have you,
For, all our joyes are but fantasticall.
And so I scape the paine, for paine is true ...

But reality wins, and the true lover cries:

Fill'd with her love, may I be rather grown
Mad with much heart, than ideott with none.

In *Lovers Infinitenesse* we will find Donne exploring the paradoxical mystery of love—with its Scriptural overtones—

> Loves riddles are, that though thy heart depart,
> It stayes at home, and thou with losing savest it.

Goodfriday, 1613, *Riding Westward*, that most moving of the Divine Poems, is based upon the paradox of the 'felix culpa', and, more precisely on St. Paul's 'autopsychopsy': 'The good that I would, I do not, but the evil that I will not, that I do.' Donne identifies the westward journey on 'pleasure or businesse' with the sinner's perversity in turning his back upon Our Lord, dying for him on the Cross;

> . . . I am carryed towards the West
> This day, When My Soules forme bends towards the East.
> There I should see a Sunne, by rising set,
> And by that setting endlesse day beget;
> But that Christ on this Crosse, did rise and fall,
> Sinne had eternally benighted all . . .

The resolution of the paradox in the closing lines demonstrates vividly and dramatically the logic of the 'felix culpa':

> O Saviour, as thou hang'st upon the tree;
> I turne my back to thee, but to receive
> Corrections, till thy mercies bid thee leave.
> O thinke mee worth thine anger, punish mee,
> Burne off my rusts, and my deformity,
> Restore thine Image, so much, by thy grace,
> That thou may'st know mee, and I'll turne my face.

In this poem we experience once again the deep emotion controlled by the ordered dialectic, and heightened by the intellectually satisfying use to which the conceit and the paradox are put. The secret of their power to convince and move us lies, not only in their choice but in Donne's rigidly logical handling of his images, keeping them to powers and modes of operation which are truly predicable of their subjects.

In the *Devotions* Donne makes the revealing confession:

> I have not the righteousness of Job, but I have the desire of Job;
> I would speake to the Almightie and I would reason with God.[18]

---

[18] *Devotions Upon Emergent Occasions*, 1624, p. 18. (quoted by H. C. White in *J. Donne and the Psychology of Spiritual Effort*, 1951).

Because of his boundless curiosity; because his intellect was equipped with the sine qua non of wit—the ability to think simultaneously on different levels, from the highest levels of abstract speculation to the lower—but still relevant—levels of ordinary living and thus to integrate in a single image or concept the whole complex of human life; and because, above all, his keen intellect searched the heart of metaphysical as well as physical reality, it was natural to him to yoke together the most heterogeneous elements he could find there, those of appearance and reality, of accident and essence, and thus it was that only through paradox could he express his profoundest convictions, the reality of his experiences in life and in love. The *First Anniversary* has a wealth of paradox:

'How witty's ruine!' is illustrated by further arresting and witty paradoxes, e.g.,

> For that first marriage was our funerall:
> One woman at one blow, then kill'd us all,
> And singly, one by one, they kill us now . . .,

and again,

> Onely death addes t'our length: nor are wee growne
> In stature to be men, till we are none.

The Crosse, and many of the Divine Poems, as well as meditations, sermons and essays are based upon some element of the Christian paradox, wittily explored and pithily expressed by Donne.

> . . . the losse
> Of this Crosse, were to mee another Crosse;
> Better were worse, for, no affliction,
> No Crosse is so extreme, as to have none.

And in his *Essays in Divinity*, speaking of the glories of the visible world, he remarks with an insight that again brings Teilhard de Chardin to mind:

> To love it too much, is to love it too little.[19]

---

[19] *Essays in Divinity*, published by Donne's son, 1651, pp. 69–72. And compare T. de Chardin, *Le Milieu Divin*, op. cit., p. 120: 'Everything means both everything and nothing to me . . . for, as the only reality which can satisfy us lies beyond the transparencies in which it is mirrored, everything that fades away and dies between us will only serve to give reality back to us with greater purity.'

For Donne with his deep spiritual insight, his respect for the real, the essences of things, and especially with his intimate experience of his own paradoxical nature it was most fitting and indeed natural for him to think in terms of the paradox.

THE PUN

Puns, like paradoxes, are very often short-cuts to truths, to levels of seriousness and of significance we might otherwise miss. The shock of the semantic coincidence vibrates through the different planes of imagination opening up for us hitherto unapprehended relations in the real order of things. The best known pun in Donne's work is the pun on his name in *A Hymne to God the Father:*

> Wilt thou forgive that sinne where I begunne,
> Which is my sin, though it were done before? . . .
> When thou hast done, thou hast not done,
> For, I have more.

The even rhythmic flow, the solemn bell-like tolling of the broad vowels and heavy stresses all help to intensify the mood of humble and genuine sorrow for sin, whilst the repetition of the pun on 'done' (for Donne) seems to emphasize his isolation from creatures and the living flux of life, in the same way that Hamlet's pun isolated him. The poem is logical, not only in structure, but in the sequence of traditional Christian prayer: Donne begging pardon, first for his own sins, then for those of others for which he may have been responsible, and finally, for that sin he dreaded most, the sin of despair:

> I have a sinne of feare, that when I have spunne
>   My last thred, I shall perish on the shore;
> Sweare by thy selfe, that at my death thy sonne
>   Shall shine as he shines now, and heretofore;
> And, having done that, Thou haste done, (i.e. Donne)
>   I feare no more.

The favourite Elizabethan pun on the coin called the 'angel' takes on new life in *The Bracelet*, the poem which Jonson admired so much, and which Leishman hails as Donne's 'most astonishingly successful exercise in sheer wit'. This rambling poem has no inconsequential lines. Bound by a stringent logic, sometimes based on the properties of gold or the accidents of the bracelet, sometimes on the traditional Christian doctrine of the Fall, or on the laws of alchemy, the mind is kept at a stretch making imaginative connections between physical and moral realms, while the entire poem is governed by the pun on the angel which is exploited in hilarious fashion by Donne:

> O shall twelve righteous Angels, which as yet
> No leaven of vile soder did admit;
> Nor yet by any way have straid or gone
> From the first state of their Creation . . .

> Shall they be damn'd, and in the furnace throwne,
> And punisht for offences not their owne?

> Thou say'st (alas) the gold doth still remaine,
> Though it be chang'd, and put into a chaine:
> So in the first falne angels, resteth still
> Wisdome and knowledge; but, 'tis turn'd to ill . . .

At the end of the poem the litany of maledictions, which still follows the logical pattern corresponding to the properties and accidents of the golden bracelet—

> Gold being the heaviest metal amongst all,
> May my most heavy curse upon thee fall:
> Here fetter'd, manacled, and hang'd in chains,
> First mayst thou bee; then chaind to hellish paines . . .—

is lightened by the trenchant humour, the 'terraefilial' sleight-of-hand of the final quatrain:

> But, I forgive; repent thee honest man:
> Gold is Restorative, restore it then:
> But if from it thou beest loath to depart,
> Because 'tis cordiall, would 'twere at thy heart.

The more we examine the conceits and the images in the poems of Donne, the more we trace them to their sources, reviving medieval doctrines and lost connotations, the more do we realize that their brilliance and wit, their power to define and to deepen experience come from the function they fulfil so perfectly in the dialectic generated from the high-powered dynamo of Donne's intelligence.

The Truth of Reality in Dialectical Balance

The reality which Donne sought to discover from the flux of experience, through his dialectic, and to explain by means of the conceit,
the paradox or the pun, was a reality compounded of matter and spirit
which took into account the complexities of the world of thought
and emotion, as well as the world of things; a metaphysical reality indeed which could have its perfect exposition only in the blinding
Image of the God of Truth Himself—the 'deep but dazzling darkness'
of which H. Vaughan writes. This is the truth which lures Donne on,
up the 'huge hill, cragged and steep', forcing him to report things as
they are in their unresolved ruggedness, denying him always the
refuge of pretence or the convenient, sycophantic service of the glib
answer. It is this intellectual honesty of his which gives the tone of
ambiguity, the sense of precarious balance to some of his best poems,
e.g. *The Nocturnall*.

In his reluctance to commit himself to any one specific attitude he
reminds us, at times, of Keats's theory of 'negative capability':

> The only means of strengthening one's intellect is to make up
> one's mind about nothing—to let the mind be a thoroughfare for
> all thoughts.[20]

The measure of Donne's—as of Keats's—greatness, lies in his recognition of the limits of his intellectual capacities. Pascal describes these
'great men':

> Knowledge has two end points which touch one another: one
> the pure, natural ignorance which all men have when they come
> into this world. At the other end are the *great men*, who, having
> traversed all human knowledge, know that they do not know,
> and come back to their original state of ignorance; this however
> is a knowing state of ignorance, an ignorance which looks
> through itself.[21]

And here we have Donne's confession:

> The ways of the Lord are past my finding out; and therefore to
> those, who doe open their eyes to that light of Nature, in the

---

[20] *The Complete Works of John Keats*, ed. H. B. Forman, 1923, Vol. V, Letter
   CXXXVII, p. 121.
[21] Quoted in *Mount Carmel*, Spring, 1962.

best exaltation thereof, God does not hide himselfe, tho' he have not manifested to me, by what way he manifests himselfe to them . . .[22]

Craig, commenting on the conception of truth in England of Donne's day, maintains that 'it suspends truth, not between hypothesis and verification, but between the affirmative and the negative in debate',[23] and that the acutest minds—such as Shakespeare's—would habitually see both sides. It is this ability not only to see both sides, but to experience both imaginatively, to be involved in both, emotionally and intellectually, and further, to be able to reproduce this vibrating tension within the confines of a poem, sometimes unresolved, sometimes achieving a very tenuous balance—this is the rare ability which sets Donne apart. And this ability to 'doubt wisely', to acknowledge other avenues of approach to truth, as well as attitudes other than the obvious, this faculty fits in with T. S. Eliot's definition of wit, which is he says—

'a recognition, implicit in the expression of every experience, of other kinds of experience which are possible.'[24]

It is this aspect of Donne's wit which may explain the sudden, and seemingly unexpected reversals, in so many of his poems, as for instance in *The Blossome, Womans Constancy, Loves Deitie, The Dampe* —poems where he seems to stop short and turn about on the tracks of his thought, asking whether the opposite of what he has just put forward and argued might not be true—

For, by to-morrow, I may thinke so too . . .
Womans Constancy.

It may be impossible to analyse this intellectual honesty, this keen steel-bright wit which pierces to the essences of things, but it is possible, I think, to point to some of the influences which shaped Donne's manner of thinking and judging, in his early days. First, there is the un-doubted influence of Aristotle, especially in his conception of dialectic as

that part of the art of discoursing which provides us with the

---

[22] Quoted by M. L. Wiley in 'Donne & the Poetry of Scepticism' *Hibbert Journ.*, Vol. XLVIII, Jan. 1950.
[23] H. Craig, *The Enchanted Glass*, 1952, Chap. VI.
[24] 'A. Marvell', *Selected Essays*, 1949, p. 300.

arguments with which we can dispute either side of a question, with a certain probability.[25]

The typical Aristotelian dialectic then does not have as its aim to convince or to confute, nor even to arrive at full certainty about the matter being discussed. It argues rather from probable premises to probable conclusions, seeking to reconcile opposites not by any illogical concessions or slick compromises but by the recognition of the truth in contrasting opinions and arguments. Lacordaire had the correct Aristotelian notion when he remarked:

> I do not seek to convince my adversary of his error, but to unite myself to him in a higher truth.

I think that the 'higher truth' Donne sought was a kind of 'Aristotelian latitude' where one could use even logically fallacious arguments in the interest of a truth not normally, or easily, perceptible to the senses or the judgment. Take, for instance, the argument at the end of *The Good-Morrow*. Here Donne makes use of at least two fallacies in the interest of a greater truth: first, the fallacy of 'secundum quid'—the application of physical standards of comparison, wherein the major premise is true—according to the old scholastic teaching:

> Whatever dyes, was not mixt equally

to a psychological and emotional state which cannot be so analysed; and, second, the fallacy 'in dictione'—of equivocation—in the use of the word 'one':

> If our two loves be one . . .

in which spiritual unity is equated with the unity of physical substances. The witty analogy which proceeds from these logically false analogies triumphantly proclaims the higher truth: that pure and reciprocated love between man and woman can live forever—

> If . . . thou and I
> Love so alike, that none doe slacken, none can die.

---

[25] W. J. Ong, *Method, Ramus & the Decay of Dialogue*, 1958, p. 216.

Similarly with *The Flea*—which Grierson tells us was so greatly admired by Donne's contemporaries as a masterpiece of wit—its meaning is below, not on, the surface. The close-knit and consecutive argument is, of course, composed of witty fallacies of all kinds, e.g., making the killing of the flea at once sacrilege, murder and suicide:

> This flea is you and I, and this
> Our mariage bed, and mariage temple is . . .

The whole wit of the poem, in fact, is based upon the sophistry of applying the same arguments to the moral as to the physical side of life, and upon the incongruity of the contrast between the high code of honour and the life-habits of one of the lowest forms of living insects.

I do not think that I would agree with Kermode[26] that the success of *The Flea* depends upon our wonder outlasting our critical attitude to the argument. Rather, I think it is when we see the world through Donne's eyes that our wonder grows. His ironic disvaluing was purposeful: the higher reality he writes about is the conduct of contemporary society in the London of the 1590s, where the loss of honour was no more to be lamented than the killing of a flea . . .

> Just so much honor, when thou yeeld'st to mee,
> Will wast, as this flea's death tooke life from thee.

Behind the bland dogmatizing, beneath the scintillating wit and the smooth sophisms, we will always find Donne the unrelenting realist.

THE ARISTOTELIAN 'MEAN'

Another quality in Donne which may be traced from his view of dialectic, but which can almost certainly be attributed to the influence of Aristotle, is his hatred of extremes of all kinds—to which reference has been made in earlier chapters—and his corresponding love for the 'via media', or, in Aristotelian language, for 'the mean'. Nobody could pursue even an elementary study of Aristotle without learning to value 'the mean' which holds such a central place in his *Ethics*.

---

[26] F. Kermode, *J. Donne*, 1957, p. 11. ('Writers & Their Work' Series, No. 86).

Virtue is a mean state between two vices, one in excess, the other
in defect . . .
The mean state is in every case praiseworthy, but that we must
incline sometimes towards excess, and sometimes towards deficiency; for thus we shall most easily hit the mean and that which is
excellent.[27]

The following quotation from the notebook of John Balderston, a
Cambridge student of the 1660s, is evidence that even at Cambridge,
and so late in the seventeenth century, the study of Aristotle and his
Ethics still held sway:

The other day we proposed a definition of virtue . . . as defined
by Aristotle elsewhere, the conscious habit (of choosing) the
mean proper to us . . .[28]

In many of his sermons and letters, as well as in his poems, Donne's
predilection for the mean is very evident. In a letter to his friend,
Henry Goodyer, defining virtue, he remarks:

He is not vertuous, out of whose actions you can pick an excellent
one . . . vices have swellings and fits and noise, because being
extreames, they dwell far asunder, and they maintain both a foreign
war against vertue, and a civill against one another . . .[29]

These lines could be taken as a homely paraphrase of Aristotle's remarks in the *Ethics*.

In *Satyre II* we find him railing against extremes such as 'Carthusian
fasts, and fulsome Bachanalls' and stating his own preference in the
stark statement: 'meanes blesse . . .'

In *The Litanie* however, we find Donne's doctrine of the mean most
fully stated. Praising this poem for its wit, Helen Gardner remarks
that it is

'startling in paradox, precise in antithesis . . . its intellectual ingenuity and verbal audacity are employed to define an ideal of
moderation in all things.'[30]

---

[27] *The Nicomachean Ethics of Aristotle*, trans. R. W. Browne, 1853, Chap. VI,
p. 45.
[28] W. T. Costello, *The Scholastic Curriculum*, 1958, p. 66.
[29] *Letters to Severall Persons of Honour*, 1651, p. 97.
[30] H. Gardner, *The Divine Poems*, 1952, Introduction.

In this poem we see the passionate and ambitious John Donne, whose worldly wisdom has betrayed him, attempting to school his own soul to patience during the trying years at Mitcham, but here, as always, he is the tough-headed and eminently sane realist:

> Lord, let us runne
> Meane waies, and call them stars, but not the Sunne;

and again in this revealing and typical stanza:

> From being anxious or secure,
> Dead clods of sadnesse, or light squibs of mirth,
> From thinking . . .
> . . . that this earth
> Is only for our prison fram'd,
> or that Thou art covetuous
> To them Thou lovest, or that they are maim'd
> From reaching this world's sweet, who seek Thee thus
> With all their might, Good Lord, deliver us.;

and, lastly, in the psychological insight of:

> When we are mov'd to seeme religious
> Only to vent wit, Good Lord deliver us.

Helen Gardner claims that *The Litanie* is the most Anglican of Donne's poems, in its pursuit of the 'via media', and in its anti-ascetic and anti-mystic bias. Again, we are faced with the problem of whether his attachment to the Anglican Church was a genuine intellectual and devotional attachment, or whether it was merely the attraction of its vaunted via media, offering him a refuge from extremes which he could not accept . . .

> I have a ridling disposition to bee ashamed of feare, and afrayd of shame . . .[31]

We note the sometimes rather strident tone of self-justification, as in *The Canonization*:

> We can dye by it, if not live by love;

---

[31] *Poetry and Prose*, Hayward, Letter to Sir H. Wotton, p. 441.

the prayer in *The Litanie* to be delivered from what he considers the extreme of fanaticism:

> . . . for oh, to some
> Not to be Martyrs, is a Martyrdome;

and the unequivocal statement in the *Preface to Pseudo-Martyr:*

> . . . to offer our lives for the defence of the Catholique Faith, hath ever beene a religious custome; but to call every pretence of the Pope, Catholique faith, and to bleede to death for it, is a sicknesse and a medicine, which the Primitive Church never understood . . .[32]

Was this the genuine conviction of the student of sacred Scripture, or the strategy of escape of the coward? Did he fasten on the Aristotelian 'mean' because it was congenial to his nature, and then use it as a shield against the sharp accusations of his own conscience? Could we diagnose his constant preoccupation with laying bare, with the scalpel of his dialectic, the reality of experience, as a 'cover-up', or compensation, for his own self-deception in this intimate matter of his conscience? Whatever the answer, Donne's sympathies are on the side of moderation, particularly as regards religion. It is interesting to note that he completely accepted Sarpi's views that the Council of Trent was too rigid and too extreme, and therefore the cause of widening instead of healing the breach between the Churches. There is no doubt that were Donne alive in these days of the Vatican II Council, he would be an enthusiastic supporter of the progressive theologians who are advocating the via media of ecumenism, and the return to the traditions of the Fathers and the early Church, which Donne himself so much desired.

Perhaps there is some significance too in the fact that the two poems by Donne's uncle, Jasper Heywood, published in *The Paradyse of Daynty Devises*, in 1578, are on this theme of prudence and moderation. Both are straightforwardly didactic—one of them ending on this significant note:

> But so climes above the meane, there is no hope of stay,
> The higher up the sooner downe, and nearer his decay.

---

[32] J. Donne, *Pseudo Martyr*, 1610.

Keeping to the mean was no easy feat in Donne's day. It required careful navigation between the quicksands of political intrigue and the rocks of contemporary religious controversy, particularly when the firm shore of authority—spiritual and temporal—was shrouded in the thick mists of doubt and fear.

Having examined the almost certain influence of Aristotle, the possible influence of his uncle, and the native influence of his own temperament and family background in Donne's predilection for the 'mean', the safe and moderate view, there is a further influence which requires comment—that of St. Thomas Aquinas. The numerous arguments from this Saint which Donne uses throughout his writings are testimony to his deep study of this giant of the Middle Ages. But Donne could not have failed to recognize a kindred spirit. St. Thomas's unrepentant realism; his intellectual hunger for knowledge of the essences of things (see footnote 4, Chapter V); his extraordinary balance of mind made evident in his dictum that 'the false is true in a certain sense'; his addiction to the Aristotelian notion of dialectic, and to arguments by means of which, as G. K. Chesterton so beautifully puts it,

> he climbed up to the turrets and talked with angels on the roofs of gold;[33]

his insistence on the application of the strict rules of logic to the symbols and the imagery of his poems; his style which Claudel describes as 'an almost literal expression of reality'; and, especially, his respect for the rôle of the senses in the life of man—all these qualities must have cried out to Donne, like deep calling to deep. But above all else, it was the Thomistic proportion which appealed to Donne: St. Thomas's doctrine of the golden mean of virtue, which sprang ultimately from his vision of God as at once transcending the universe in His unique perfection, and immanent in it by His Providence and knowledge; and historically, from his acceptance of the Aristotelian principles in his philosophy.

Our poet must have been familiar too with St. Thomas's definition of beauty as expressed in the *Summa Theologica*. It is here that we can discern another influence on Donne's preoccupation with the mean or proportion. The three requisites for beauty listed by St. Thomas

---

[33] *St. Thomas Aquinas*, 1938 p. 216.

are: integrity, proportion and radiance. In the *First Anniversary*, we find Donne describing the decay of the world in these exact terms:

> For the worlds beauty is decai'd, or gone,
> Beauty, that's colour, and proportion.

Colour here, of course, stands for radiance. Later in the poem Donne makes proportion the fundamental principle of beauty:

> And, oh, it can no more be questioned,
> That beauties best, proportion, is dead.

The Thomistic 'proportion', the Aristotelian 'mean', the via media— call it what you will—it is this quality in Donne which becomes the touchstone of the truth he seeks through his dialectic, preserving it from the distortion of the idealist; and it is this which, in turn, gives credibility to his realism, saving it (except perhaps in some verses in the *Elegies* and the *Satyres*) from the extreme of carnality and the depravity of cynicism.

DONNE'S VISION OF REALITY

We have seen how Donne uses the dialectic method, and its tool, the metaphysical image, to grapple with reality, to lay bare the subtle manoeuvrings of the human heart and to prick the bubble of a moral smugness which would take no account of reality. We have also seen that reality to Donne was the whole complex life of man in the context of this fallen world, where everything is 'quite out of joynt', and where there are no set formulae for the resolving of life's problems. Hence it is that very rarely in Donne's poems, and never in his best, will we find easy solutions or pat answers to the arguments in question. Instead we have the opposing forces—opinions, emotions, facts unrefined and often unrelated—brought healthily into the open, clinically dissected by his scathing wit and searching dialectic, and thus analysed and aired allowed to settle in a kind of precarious and precious balance. He is never dogmatic, never didactic. The tension in his best poems is at once a result of the Aristotelian latitude of his mind which can entertain contrary opinions and emotions simultaneously, a testimony to the honesty of the intellect which gives such urgency to his dialectic, and a measure of the passion with which he longed for the metaphysical perfection of the pre-Fall state, which at once haunted and lured him on.

I like to think of Donne as a very able judge summoning to the bar of his wit every shade of opinion, every nuance of feeling, every accepted cliché, now cross-examining or cajoling, again deftly parrying thrusts, or swiftly striking home, while we in the audience wait excitedly for a sentence which never comes. Instead he gives us the vision of reality which he himself wins through the patient exercise of his dialectic—the vision that holds in balance all the complexity of life: the good and the bad, the simple and the difficult, the material and the spiritual, in the human situation. With Donne we are privileged —as Wallace Stevens has succinctly put it—to walk 'barefoot into reality'.

The poems which follow are chosen because they illustrate what Thomas Carew meant by Donne's 'line of masculine expression': his ability to portray by means of the toughly masculine technique of dialectical reasoning, and of compressed images which detonate into the fields of philosophy, science and religion 'that which is in the thrust of a quivering glance' (St. Augustine)—the uncertainties, the tensions, the self-deceptions, the ambiguities which are the very stuff of human life and love.

Love's Growth: In this poem Donne examines the contradictory nature of his own experience in love. If, as his intimate evidence reveals, love is not an 'ever-fixéd mark', but waxes and wanes, allures and repels, how, he asks, can it be the spiritual thing he had always believed it to be? We note how the delightful wit aerates the dialectic, giving a new dimension to the old scholastic doctrine concerning the purity of all spiritual substances—

> Love's not so pure, and abstract, as they use
> To say, which have no Mistresse but their Muse . . .;

and his conclusion, so satisfyingly logical, so appropriate, yet so evocative of transcendental values:

> But as all else, being elemented too,
> Love sometimes would contemplate, sometimes do.

The next stanza is Donne's exposition of this thesis. By means of Springtime images he tries to show that such 'vicissitudes and seasons' do not deny the eternal, unchanging, spiritual nature of his love.

> And yet no greater, but more eminent,
> Love by the Spring is growne . . .

Just as the greater intensity of light, reflected by the stars at this time, declare the closer proximity of the changeless sun; and just as the blossoms on the bough are but evidence of the greater intensity of life in the hidden root, so, he decides, the gentler Springtime manifestations of his love—

> love . . . would . . . sometimes do

do but prove the vigour of its inner growth, its spiritual, as contrasted with its sensual energy:

> Gentle love deeds, as blossomes on a bough,
> From love's awakened root do bud out now . . .

But neither Donne nor the reader is deceived by the sophistry of the argument. He does not prove what he set out to prove: that

> love is not love
> Which alters when it alteration finds . . .

He is however more honest, more realistic than Shakespeare in this particular sonnet. Human love, this side the grave, he seems to say, can have but a seasonal beauty, a temporary intensity.

It is very interesting to note how the last four lines of the poem seem to contradict Donne's earlier conclusion—that a more demonstrative love, symbolized by springtime growth, does not necessarily signify an increase in love, when he declares:

> And though each spring doe adde to love new heate . . .
> No winter shall abate the springs increase.

One would have expected the more logical conclusion: an emphasis on the fact that the undemonstrative, contemplative type of love— Ben Jonson's 'little winter-love'—has at least the same spiritual intensity as the less inhibited, the more effervescent Springtime-type. I think the clue to the riddle is to be found in the difficult analogy of the Prince, who, during the wintertime of peace and inaction still continues to exact wartime taxes—taxes which, though meaningless in the circumstances, still strengthen, add growth, to his Treasury:

> As princes doe in times of action get
> New taxes, and remit them not in peace . . .

This is Donne's way of realistically stating the necessity all human love has, no matter how spiritual its core, of expressing itself by human ways and means. Love, he declares triumphantly, though spiritual in essence, does grow, and grows by unspiritual i.e., by the help of physical and sensual means: Springtime blossoms on a bough; sensible manifestations and demonstrations. 'Why not?' Donne will ask in a later poem—

> Else a great Prince in prison lies . . .
>   *The Extasie*

In *Lovers Infinitenesse* we have another investigation of the nature of love, using logic, lawyers' terminology and paradox in an effort to arrive at a resolution. Having at the end of stanza two won the right to possess all the love of his beloved—

> . . . thy heart is mine, what ever shall
> Grow there, deare, I should have it all . . .

7

he suddenly reverses the argument, declaring:

> Yet I would not have all yet . . . ,

bolstering his new position with ingenious though—seemingly—irrefutably logical arguments:

> Thou canst not every day give me thy heart,
> If thou canst give it, then thou never gavest it . . .

Then, having clenched this point by means of the paradox:

> . . . that though thy heart depart,
> It stayes at home, and thou with losing savest it

he summarily rejects both judgments to find 'Lovers Infinitenesse' in a mutual trusting love:

> . . . so wee shall
> Be one, and one anothers All.

This neat solution to the dilemma does not, however, fully resolve the questions raised in the first two stanzas by Donne. Nor did he intend it to do so—as is evidenced by his use of the word 'but' immediately following on the paradox. The truth about love which he is concerned to portray in this poem is, that since on neither side their love is perfect—being more concerned with receiving than with giving—the only way to preserve it is to

> . . . have a way more liberall,
> Than changing hearts, to joyne them, so wee shall
> Be one, and one anothers All.

i.e., the acceptance of the beloved with all the human limitations of his or her nature. Love is never treated as an idealized state with Donne. The solution to the arguments raised by this poem could be expressed only in infinity: in a relationship which belongs to time yet transcends it; which is always a-making, like an ocean with tides ebbing and flowing from the spirit, the flesh and the intellect, and salted by the vitality of each in the common shared life, the union where neither is lover nor beloved, giver nor receiver, but 'each is indistinguishably both.'

The Nocturnall: There is uncertainty both about the dating of this poem and about the person for whom it was composed. Leishman thinks that it was written for Donne's wife, who was he claims, if not actually, at least anticipatedly dead. Grierson, however, holds that it was written for Lucy, Countess of Bedford, possibly during her severe illness of 1612. Whatever one decides, the 'Lucy' of this poem does stand for all that Donne ever loved, for all that gave meaning to life for him. Of all his poems it gives the most immediate account of an experience being lived through. It is, perhaps, the best illustration of Donne's power to hold antithetical notions in a balanced tension which is vibrant with passion.

Grierson holds that the subject of the poem is 'the emptiness of life without love.' But it is about more than mere emptiness: it is about retrogression on the metaphysical plane of being: a reversion to primeval chaos, and in this concept lies the key to the whole dilemma. For though primeval chaos inspires more terror and suggests a greater upheaval in terms of the cosmos, than does mere emptiness, it yet holds within it the germ of a new creation. Though its subject could, at first glance, be appropriately named 'Death-in-Life', as the poem progresses there is a subtle change of tone and emphasis which would seem to suggest, and to justify, a change of the title to 'Life-in-Death'.

One does not know what to marvel at most: the faultless dialectical reasoning, the aptness of the philosophical terms used in the images, the strictly logical structure, or the almost palpable tone of indecision which is yet allied to a perfectly balanced ending. One feels that in this instance Donne made a poem which is an 'objective correlative' for his own subtle heart, forever restlessly questioning, controlled only by the logic of his realism.

In *The Nocturnall* Donne identifies life with love. Hence, with the death of love he is 'ruin'd', in the old philosophical meaning of the word, i.e. robbed of 'form', of soul, of meaning. Now he is but matter

> . . . rebegot
> Of absence, darknesse, death; things which are not.

From matter he descends to chaos, and, finally, he is

> of the first nothing, the Elixer grown.

Here, in the dead hour of midnight, in the year's winter, the unreality

of life without love, without hope, takes possession of him. The numb-
ness of despair is wonderfully portrayed by his checking of himself, in
strict logical fashion, for the rôles which belong in the realm of being:

> Were I a man, that I were one,
> I needs must know; I should preferre,
> If I were any beast,
> Some ends, some means; Yea plants, yea stones detest,
> And love; All, all some properties invest . . .

Without intelligence, feeling, or the will to live, he is indeed the
'quintessence of nothingnesse'. But here, in the final paragraph, we
have the ambiguity which gives such conviction to the poem. William
Empson points out that

> Ambiguity . . . occurs when two or more meanings of a statement
> do not agree among themselves, but combine to make clear a
> more complicated state of mind in the author.[34]

Thus Donne's complicated state of mind and confused feelings come
wonderfully across to us, from the ambiguity in the ideas of chaos
and nothingness which he stresses. Speaking of the Aristotelian notion
of privation—or nothingness—Etienne Gilson says that it

> points out the nonbeing of something that ought to be . . .
> . . . the absence of something that should be there . . . ,[35]

And that this was the connotation Donne had in mind is borne out
by the content of the poem. In the same way the word 'chaos' is
associated both with destruction and with the primeval chaos which
preceded creation.

Donne fully realizes that the life he knew is ended; that the world
he shared with his beloved has disintegrated; yet he is too hardy a
realist to deny entirely the hope of another life, in a different kind of
world. So, while the last stanza begins with the despairing sonor-
ousness of

> But I am None . . . ,

---

[34] W. Empson, *Seven Types of Ambiguity*, 1961, p. 133.
[35] E. Gilson, *Painting and Reality*, 1958, p. 106.

and the bitter comparison of his sunless life with the Summer of
other lovers, yet as the stanza progresses we find that the long dark
night of the opening lines of the poem has become the forward-
looking vigil, the Eve to a feast of sacred love, the promise of a new
life which is to follow:

> Let mee prepare towards her, and let mee call
> This houre her Vigill, and her Eve, since this
> Both the yeares, and the dayes deep midnight is.

The promise of the new life is implicit also in the ambiguity which
attaches to the word 'Eve', bringing echoes from the Garden of Eden
and the dawn of our creation.

But once again we must note that there is no definite resolution
of the conflict here. As Richard Sleight sums up in the best commentary I have read on *The Nocturnall*,

> Reintegration or relapse must seem equally possible almost to
> the end . . . He (Donne) does not definitely commit himself to the
> harmony of death nor to the dialectic of being.[36]

Few poets, other than Shakespeare or Keats, have so laid bare the
'naked, thinking heart'; few have made so palpable the sense of unreality—of being cut off from all species—which pervades man's being
when in the grip of despair; fewer still have reported it with the
psychological accuracy of Donne.

In this poem he is supremely the poet-dialectician of metaphysical
reality—one could say too of unreality—using images from philosophy,
science and alchemy, according to the strict logic of their terms, to
give authentic utterance to an experience, so intimate and deeply-felt
that it borders on the ineffable.

The First Anniversary—An Anatomy of the World: The rich ambiguity
of this poem has successively puzzled students of Donne down the
years, from its first critic, Ben Jonson, whose remarks are recorded for
us by Drummond:

> That Dones Anniversarie was profane and full of blasphemies;
> that he told Mr. Donne, if it had been written of the Virgin Mary

---

[36] *Interpretations*, ed. J. Wain, 1955, p. 49.

it had been something; to which he answered, that he described
the Idea of a Woman, and not as she was.[37]

Most critics complain of the haphazard nature of the poem, with the
brilliant exception of Martz, who declares that both *Anniversaries* are
carefully designed, though he admits that the *First* is successful only in
isolated patches, and lacks unity. The failure to understand the *First
Anniversary* is due chiefly to the paradoxical nature of its subject.
Donne himself tells us that it is not a mere eulogy of a girl he never
knew, but rather the contrast of the ideal with the real: the 'Idea of a
Woman' embodying his ideals of a pre-Fall, a Paradisal perfection,
where all is integrity, proportion and radiance, contrasted with the
real, contemporary world, which is described, not only in eloquent
phrases such as these:

> our age was Iron and rustie too . . .

and

> Then, as mankinde, so is the worlds whole frame
> Quite out of joynt, almost created lame . . .

or, the oft quoted—

> 'Tis all in pieces, all cohaerence gone

but more pertinently, though more subtly, by means of the paradoxes
and ambiguities, and even the absurdities, which so surely reflect
the complexity, and the seeming meaninglessness of our lives here
below:

> Wee seem ambitious, Gods whole worke t'undoe;
> Of nothing Hee made us, and we strive too,
> To bring ourselves to nothing back . . .;

and

> For every man alone thinkes he hath got
> To be a Phoenix, and that then can bee
> None of that kinde, of which he is, but hee;

---

[37] *Conversations with Drummond of Hawthornden*, op. cit, p. 5.

or,

> Be more than man, or thou'rt lesse than an Ant . . .

If the poem seems disjointed, and if we weary of the endless repetition
of arguments, we should remember that we are assisting at the anatomizing of the world, in the hope as Donne expresses it, that

> This new world may be safer, being told
> The dangers and diseases of the old.

It is however a tiresome operation, acknowledged so by Donne:

> But as in cutting up a man that's dead,
> The body will not last out . . .

> So the worlds carcase would not last, if I
> Were punctuall in this Anatomy;
> Not smels it well to hearers, if one tell
> Them their disease, who faine would think they're well.

Here it could not be said that the realism had been set to music by the
poet. It is not that Donne has been carried away by his anatomizing
effort, but rather that he is kept earthbound by a piece of 'sett musike'—
he whose soul delighted in a 'voluntary'. The ambiguities and the
grimness seem to be more emphasized and laboured over than presented
to us through the 'window on the infinite' which art should provide—
except when Donne's imagination is suddenly fired by a reflection on
the bewildering flux in contemporary conditions, as here:

> The sun is lost, and th'earth, and no mans wit
> Can well direct him where to looke for it.
> . . . the Firmament

> Is crumbled out againe to his Atomies.
> 'Tis all in peeces, all cohaerence gone;
> All just supply, and all Relation . . .;

or when his vision seeks to penetrate and express the perfected happiness of the resurrected spirit:

> She's now a part both of the Quire, and Song . . .

He is sometimes uncharacteristically didactic:

> nothing
> Is worth our travaile, griefe, or perishing,
> But those rich joyes, which did possesse her heart,
> Of which she's now partaker, and a part . . .

This last line with its confusing of active and passive, of part with whole, admirably illustrates Donne's aim throughout the poem, which is to portray the confusion and the paradox of man's fallen state:

> This man, so great, that all that is, is his,
> Oh what a trifle, and poore thing he is . . .

The dialectic is difficult to trace throughout, but perhaps in this instance it could with justice be called the 'dialectic of confusion', as Donne endeavours to steady the rambling poem on its course towards his vision of metaphysical perfection and harmony. It is the forced note which spoils the poem. It is as if Donne were conscious of his patron peering over his shoulder as he wrote—to the distraction of his Muse, and sometimes, to the prostitution of his poetic powers.

THE DIALECTIC OF THE SERMONS

The dialectic of Donne's prose works, and in particular of the sermons, has still the unmistakable Donnean characteristics of syllogistic reasoning, strengthened by analogy, and accompanied by detailed and original analysis, but now more copiously illustrated by 'exempla' which are often startling in their naïvety. The passion is there too, kindling the crowding ideas which seem to catch fire from one another, for Donne, even in the pulpit, could never be a mere commentator on some dry academic text. On his lips it comes to life, impregnated by his dynamism, fired with the intensity of his emotion, made comprehensible and compelling by the personal experience from the heart of which Donne always writes and speaks.

In most of his sermons Donne follows the method of precise definition and illuminating analysis, leading up to an exalted climax. Take for instance, his sermon at St. Paul's in the early 1620s, based on the text: 'Let us rejoice and be glad all our days'. Here Donne opens with a general definition which fulfils the double function of introducing his subject and forestalling the objections of those who would question its applicability to 'all our days'—in particular to days of shipwreck or other misfortune of an outward nature, or to days of inward remorse and grief of spirit—by stating unequivocally the true source of this joy, his own firm belief that

> God shall never take from me . . . my internal gladnesse and consolation, in his undeceivable and undeceiving spirit, that He is mine and I am his . . .

He then goes on to apply the text to all the various days of a man's life: the days of youth and of age; the days of mirth and the midnights of sadness; and finally, the days of death and judgment, illustrating each step in the analysis with arguments drawn from the Old Testament, and from the Fathers, Basil and Chrysostom, and with such original and dramatic figures as these:

> . . . as the Sunne may say to the starres at Nonne, How frivoulous and impertinent a thing is your light now? So this joy shall say unto laughter, Thou art mad, and unto mirth, What dost thou?

But more striking than the logic and the learning, and the appositeness of the metaphors, is the urgency of Donne's personal conviction which

is palpably conveyed to us through the streaming sentences and clauses
which flow, unchecked by any real rests in the punctuation, through
the limpid length of the sermon, to reach a climax of eloquence which
is at once both a logical summary and an expression of a deep, living
faith:

> In omnibus diebus, in all these dayes, the dayes of youth, and the
> wantonnesses of that, the dayes of age, and the tastlesnesse of that,
> the days of mirth, and the sportfulnesse of that, and of inordinate
> melancholy, and the disconsolatnesse of that... in the day of Death,
> which pieces up that circle, and in that day which enters another
> circle that hath no pieces, but is one equall everlastingnesse, the
> day of Judgment, Either I shall rejoyce, be able to declare my faith,
> and zeale to the assistance of others, or at least be glad in mine
> owne heart, in a firme hope of mine owne salvation.[38]

We note again, at the end of a later sermon on the ubiquity and
universality of God's mercies to man, how the tapestry woven by
Donne from the warp and woof of the logical analyses made throughout the passage, is given warmth and colour by the sheer intensity of
his feeling:

> But God hath made no decree to distinguish the seasons of his
> mercies; In paradise the fruits were ripe, the first minute, and in
> heaven it is alwaies Autumne, his mercies are ever in their maturity
> ... He can bring thy Summer out of Winter, though thou have no
> Spring; though in the wayes of fortune, or understanding, or
> conscience, thou have been benighted till now, wintred and
> frozen, clouded and eclypsed, damped and benummed, smothered
> and stupefied till now, now God comes to thee, not as in the
> dawning of the day, not as in the bud of the Spring, but as the
> Sun at noon to illustrate all shadowes, as the sheaves in harvest, to
> fill all penuries, all occasions invite his mercies, and all times are
> his seasons.[39]

Though we are all the time very much aware of Donne's serious and
personal involvement in the sermons, we are not perhaps, drawn into
the vortex of his passion nor made to feel the quivering immediacy

---

[38] *Poetry & Prose*, Hayward, op. cit., pp. 667–671.
[39] Ibid., p. 586.

of the experience. We miss the tension and the ambiguities, the straining after integrity, the longing for assurance and security which give
a timelessness, an ever-youthful energy to his greatest poems. We have
the feeling that the warfare is done; the journey is over; that Donne has
arrived. We find that the dialectic of his sermons is therefore used by
him more for exposition than for exploration, and to this end he
employs the numerous 'exempla', as well as the battery of repetitive
questions, within which the frequent occurrence of assonance and
alliteration, together with the subtle minor shock of the off-vowelling
act like a persistent knell:

> . . . may not thy acres, thy miles, thy shires shrink into feet, and
> so few feet, as shall but make up thy grave? . . .[40]

and again:

> In what wrinkle, in what furrow, in what bowel of the earth,
> ly all the grains of the ashes of a body burnt a thousand years
> since?[41]

Indeed in the sermons much more than in the poetry, Donne combines
with his own sensuous and original style of writing, all the music
and splendour of the speech of that great age made immortal by
Shakespeare and his peers.

It is still, however, the dialectic of reality, and it is this fact which
distinguishes the sermons of Donne from those of other seventeenth
century divines such as Sir Thomas Browne and Jeremy Taylor
which impress us more by their learned references, their often self-
conscious style, and their spare dialectic than by the living truth of
the text, and its practical value in our lives. Time and again Donne
brings the most rarefied theological arguments to earth, to a practical
application to daily life, by means of everyday idioms and homely
imagery.

Here are doctrines illustrated by references familiar to every house-
wife:

> All eggs are not hatched that the hen sits upon; neither could
> Christ himselfe get all the chickens that were hatched, to come,
> and to stay under his wings . . .[42]

---

[40] *Poetry & Prose*, Hayward, op. cit., p. 578.
[41] Ibid., p. 683.
[42] Ibid., p. 594.

and again:

> God windes us off the skein, that he may weave us into the whole
> peece, and he cuts us out of the whole peece into peeces, that he
> may make us up into a whole garment . . .[43]

Nature images, so rare in his poetry, are used to give point to his sermon on Death the leveller:

> The ashes of an Oak in the Chimney are no Epitaph of that
> Oak, to tell me how high or how large it was; it tels me not what
> flocks it sheltered while it stood, nor what men hurt it when it
> fell . . . and when a whirle-wind hath blowne the dust of the
> Church-yard into the Church . . . who will undertake to sift those
> dusts again, and to pronounce, This is the Patrician, this is the
> noble flowre, and this the yeomanly, this the Plebeian bran . . .;[44]

and to his sermon on purity of heart:

> Let him that is subject to these smaller sins, remember, that as a
> spider builds always where he knows there is most access and
> haunt of flies, so the Devil that hath cast these light cobwebs
> into thy heart, knows that that heart is made of vanities and
> levities . . .[45]

An image from the contemporary scene gives added sharpness to his
words on a favourite theme:

> . . . all our life is but a going out to the place of execution, to
> death. Now was there ever any man seen to sleep in the cart,
> between Newgate and Tyborne? . . . and we sleep all the way;
> from the womb to the grave we are never thoroughly awake . . .[46]

In a significant passage Donne surveys his conduct during prayer,
with wry humour, piercing our consciousness, as it were, with the
sensible detail, the particularity of the sharp straw:

> I throw my selfe downe in my chamber, and I call in, and invite

---

[43] *Poetry & Prose*, Hayward, p. 600.
[44] Ibid., p. 603.
[45] Ibid., p. 734.
[46] Ibid., p. 615.

God, and his Angels thither, and when they are there, I neglect
God and his Angels, for the noise of a Flie, for the ratling of a
Coach, for the whining of a doore; I talke on, in the same posture
of praying; Eyes lifted up; knees bowed downe; as though I
prayed to God; and if God, or his Angels should aske me, when
I last thought of God in that prayer, I cannot tell . . . A memory of
yesterdays pleasure, a feare of to-morrows dangers, a straw under
my knee, a noise in mine eare . . . troubles me in my prayer . . .[47]

The emotional power of this justly famous passage from the *Devotions*
is due as much to the clear logic of the dialectic, which is made convincing by its concrete everyday imagery, as to the sonorous music
and the dignity of the rhythm:

The Bell doth toll for him that thinkes it doth . . . No man is an
Iland, intire of it selfe; every man is a peece of the Continent, a
part of the maine; if a Clod bee washed away by the Sea, Europe
is the lesse, as well as if a Promontorie were, as well as if a Mannor
of thy friends or of thine owne were; any mans death diminishes
me, because I am involved in Mankinde; and therefore never
send to know for whom the bell tolls; It tolls for thee . . .[48]

Since the circle was the usual Elizabethan and Jacobean symbol for
what is perfect and eternal, it is natural to find Donne employing it
frequently throughout his sermons to signify God. We note however
the original and arresting development of ideas, springing from this
concept:

One of the most convenient Hieroglyphicks of God, is a Circle;
and a Circle is endlesse; whom God loves, hee loves to the end . . .
His hailstones, and his thunderbolts . . . (emblemes and instruments of his Judgements) fall downe in a direct line, and affect
and strike some one person, or place: His Sun, and Moone and
Starres (Emblemes and Instruments of his Blessings) move cir-
cularly, and communicate themselves to all . . .[49]

and in the *Devotions* he uses the same image in a yet more compelling
dialectic:

As hee that would describe a circle in paper, if hee have brought

---

[47] *Poetry & Prose*, Hayward, p. 673.
[48] Ibid., p. 538.
[49] L. P. Smith, *Donne's Sermons*, 1919, p. 134.

that circle within one inch of finishing, yet if he remove his compasse, he cannot make it up a perfit circle, except he fall to work
again, to finde out the same centre, so, though setting that foot of
my compasse upon thee, I have gone so farre, as to the considera-
tion of my selfe, yet if I depart from thee, my center, all is
unperfit.[50]

From the contemplation of the infinitude and perfection of the God-
head, Donne turns to consider the reality of man's fallen state, using
as symbol for man's 'off-centred' being, and wavering heart, the
perfect image of the mariner's compass:

> A perfect rectitude we cannot have in any wayes in this world . . .
> A Compasse is a necessary thing in a Ship, and the helpe of that
> Compasse brings the Ship home safe, and yet that Compasse
> hath some variations, it doth not looke directly North . . . He that
> comes as neere uprightnesse, as infirmities admit, is an upright
> man, though he have some obliquities . . .[51]

It will readily be seen that Donne's images in the *Sermons*, and in the
Devotions, serve a different function to that which they served in the
poetry. Though still strengthening and illuminating the dialectic of the
real they are no longer used as metaphysical tools to explore that
reality, to discover new relationships, but rather as parables, or as
'allegories in little', to rediscover old truths and make them memorable. It was not the novelty nor the ingenuity of the imagery which
caught the attention of his audience, but rather the forcefulness which
they lent to the dialectic, and the wonderful everyday significance
which they gave to the great truths of Christianity.

Donne's favourite themes—particularly in the Sermons—have to
do with the stark realities of life and death: the insufficiency, the
transitoriness, the imperfection of man's nature and of all temporal
things; the certainty of death and the mockery its gruesome details
offer to our pretensions. Many critics consider Donne's dwelling on
details connected with the grave, in particular with the activities of the
worm, as evidence of a certain morbid propensity in his make-up.
It is not so much morbidity however as his cult of reality brought to
extremes. They are indeed hard facts, and perhaps what makes them

---

[50] *Devotions Upon Emergent Occasions*, ed. J. Sparrow, 1923, pp. 123–4.
[51] *Poetry & Prose*, Hayward, op. cit., p. 649.

bearable is the constant impenetration, at all levels, of the grace and sweetness of the theological virtues, so strong and living in Donne: his deep faith, his hope in God's mercy, his belief in His love. In a sermon delivered 'At the Earl of Bridgewaters house in London at the marriage of his daughter. November, 19th, 1627', we find Donne speaking of the loathesome details inseparable from death and decay. Incongruous and morbid? It is so only when considered outside of its context. Within, it furnishes the discord which heightens—throws into greater relief—the harmony which follows:

> . . . and then all dies, and all dries, and molders into dust, and that dust is blowen into the river, and that puddled water tumbled into the sea, and that ebs and flows in infinite revolutions, and still, still God knows in what Cabinet every seed-Pearle lies, in what part of the world every graine of every mans dust lies; and sibilat populum suum . . . he whispers, he hisses, he beckens for the bodies of his Saints, and in the twinckling of an eye, that body that was scattered over all the elements, is sate down at the right hand of God, in a glorious resurrection . . .[52]

It is small wonder indeed that whether at a marriage or a funeral, whether at Whitehall or at St. Paul's, Donne's sermons could

> hold a London congregation enthralled, unwearied, unsatiated . . . And this congregation consisted, both of the people down to the lowest, and of the most noble, wise, accomplished of that highly intellectual age. They sat, even stood, undisturbed, except by their own murmurs of admiration, sometimes by hardly suppressed tears.[53]

Donne's power to evoke the appropriate, indeed almost the actual physical sensation, by the choice and the alliance of his words is another means used by him to translate theory into the reality of everyday experience. In this, as in so many other characteristics, he reminds one forcibly of G. M. Hopkins. Note the force of the verbs here, in their massed strength suggesting the tentacle-hold of the insinuating, enfolding, debilitating habits of sin:

> . . . howsoever thine habituall, and customary, and concatenated

---

[52] *Poetry & Prose*, Hayward, op. cit., p. 683.
[53] H. H. Milman, *Annals of S. Paul's Cathedral*, 2nd ed., 1869, p. 328 (quoted by L. P. Smith in *Donne's Sermons*).

sins, sin enwrapped and complicated in sin, sin entrenched and
barricadoed in sin, sin screwed up, and riveted with sin, may
stand out . . .[54]

Other passages owe their power of conviction to the frequent repetition
of key words, in a solemn and rhythmic context:

> When he who was a great lord, must be but a cottager, and not so
> wel; for a cottager must have so many acres to his cottage: but
> in this case, a little piece of an acre, five-foot, is become the house
> itself; the house and the land; the grave is all: lower than that the
> grave is the land, and the tenement, and the tenant too . . .[55]

Paradox and pun, internal chiming and vigorous metaphors give
emotional and intellectual force to the following lines:

> . . . though the sins which thou hast done, cannot be undone, yet
> neither shalt thou bee undone by them; There, where thou art
> afraid of them, in judgement, they shall never meet thee; but as in
> the round frame of the World, the farthest West is East, where the
> West ends, the East begins, so in thee (who art a world too) thy
> West and thy East shall joyne, and when thy Sun, thy soule comes
> to set in thy death-bed, the Son of grace shall suck it up into
> glory.[56]

We can almost hear the living timbre of Donne's voice in such passages, and in dramatic sequences such as the following:

> Poore intricated soule! Riddling, perplexed, labyrinthicall soule!
> . . . If there were no God, thou couldest not speake, thou couldest
> not thinke . . . I respit thee but a few houres, but six houres, but
> till midnight. Wake then; and then darke, and alone, heare God
> aske thee then, remember that I asked thee now, Is there a God?
> and if thou darest, say No.[57]

The dialectic in the sermons, and to a lesser extent in his controversial
works, and in the *Devotions Upon Emergent Occasions*, is, by the very

[54] *Poetry & Prose*, Hayward, op. cit., p. 631.
[55] Ibid., p. 578.
[56] Ibid., p. 624.
[57] Ibid., p. 628.

requirements of its medium, more fluid than in the poems. It is less concentrated, less convoluted, less witty, and one could perhaps say less pure, since it freely borrows the devices of rhetoric and of poetry, and makes use of a looser structure which sometimes seems to dissipate the energy of the argument. But in essentials it is the same dialectic; in it the whole of Donne's being is engaged, heart and intellect, senses and emotions, body and soul, not now to grapple with reality, nor to achieve a precarious peace between contending powers of mind and body, but to demonstrate logically, and with all the sincerity of his sensitive nature, the true reality of man's life, its ultimate meaning, when viewed from the perspective of eternity.

It is Donne's passionate sincerity which fires the dry scriptural exegesis, and bends and moulds the dialectic, until within it we can recognize the voice of one who is indeed 'involved in mankind'. His preaching is at opposite poles from that to which we in our life time have been too often accustomed: 'arid, doctrinally correct sermons . . . too abstract, too untouched by life—by the lives of individual preachers to begin with.'[58]

'How little of a Man is the Heart', comments Donne in the *Devotions*, 'and yet it is all, by which he is.'[59]
Donne's heart and life were in his preaching. We note the frank intimacy as well as the modern subtlety of self-analysis, in such lines as these:

> I am not all here, I am here now preaching upon this text, and I am at home in my Library considering whether S. Gregory, or S. Hierome, have said best of this text, before. I am here speaking to you, and yet I consider by the way, in the same instant, what it is likely you will say to one another, when I have done . . .[60]

At all times he speaks in moving personal terms of his own experience, his own sinfulness, his confidence in God's love and mercy.

> The contemplation of God, and heaven, is a kinde of buriall . . . and in this death of rapture, and extasie, in this death of the Contemplation of my interest in my Saviour, I shall finde my self, and all my sins enterred, and entombed in his wounds, and like a Lily

---

[58] *Herder Correspondence*, Vol. I, No. 11, Nov. 1964. 'Time of Decision for Irish Catholicism.'

[59] *Poetry & Prose*, Hayward, op. cit., p. 527.

[60] Quoted by L. P. Smith, *Donne's Sermons*, 1919, p. 3.

in Paradise, out of red earth, I shall see my soule rise out of his blade, in a candor, and in an innocence, contracted there, acceptable in the sight of his Father.[61]

It is the ringing sincerity of Donne's personal voice which held his audiences enthralled. It is to this quality that Walton pays tribute when he describes Donne as

> preaching the Word so, as shewed his own heart was possessed with those very thoughts, and joys that he labored to distill into others . . . always preaching to himself, like an Angel from a cloud, but in none . . .;[62]

and it is of this same personal quality that Grierson is thinking when he writes:

> . . . Donne is most eloquent when, escaping from dogmatic minutiae and controversial 'points', he appeals directly to the heart and conscience. A reader may care little for the details of seventeenth century theology and yet enjoy without qualification Donne's fervid and original thinking, and the figurative richness, and splendid harmonies of his prose in passages of argument, of exhortation and of exalted meditation. It is Donne the poet who transcends every disadvantage of theme and method . . . There are sentences in the sermons which, in beauty of imagery and cadence, are not surpassed by anything he wrote in verse, or by any prose of the century from Hooker's to Sir Thomas Browne's.[63]

The secret of Donne's appeal, in the seventeenth as in the twentieth century, lies in the steadfastness and the reality of his vision of man's life, and its meaning 'sub specie aeternitatis'.

> If every gnat that flies were an Arch-angell, all that could but tell me, that there is a God; and the poorest worme that creeps, tells me that . . . all things that are, are equally removed from being nothing; and whatsoever hath any beeing, is by that very beeing, a glasse in which we see God, who is the roote, and the fountaine of all beeing . . .[64]

---

[61] Quoted by L. P. Smith, op. cit., p. 203.
[62] *Walton's Lives*, 1903, 'Life of Dr. J. Donne', p. 38.
[63] H. J. C. Grierson, *Cambridge History of Literature*, IV, 220–1.
[64] *Poetry & Prose*, Hayward, op. cit., p. 611.

SUMMARY

We have studied in this Chapter the 'raison d'être' of Donne's dialectic: his hunger for a metaphysical knowledge of reality, a knowledge which would explain his own nature to himself in terms satisfying to his senses and to his intelligence, and in relation to the milieu in which he lived. His methods have been illustrated chiefly from the poems and the sermons, because in these we hear most clearly the authentic ring of his voice. Perhaps the most striking fact which has emerged from our analysis is the great honesty of Donne's intellect, which prevents him at all times from putting consistency before truth, or from pandering to our susceptibilities by covering up the natural and the real with the false cloak of convention. As has already been remarked, such respect for the nature of things, especially for the nature of the human heart and the human situation, must be traced to Donne's deeply sensitive and profoundly spiritual nature. In a sermon preached at St. Paul's in 1622, he remarks that

> . . . as a ship that lies in harbour within land, sometimes needs most of the points of the Compasse, to bring her forth: so if a man surrender himselfe wholly to the opinion of other men, and have not his Criterium, his touchstone within him, he will need both North and South, all the points of the Compasse, the breath of all men . . .[65]

Donne had his criterion, his touchstone, in his life-long pursuit of the truth in things, the truth which was not only the image, but very part of Very Truth Itself.

---

[65] *Poetry & Prose*, Hayward, op. cit., p. 714.

'Nothing else is . . .'

The Sunne Rising

CHAPTER V

THE DIALECTIC OF SOUL AND BODY
IN THE LOVE POEMS

DONNE was the first major English poet to treat of love as a wholly
natural passion; a passion in which body and soul have their part; in
which union of hearts does not mean identification of personality—
of desires, tastes and outlook—but the acceptance of divergent attitudes
and moods, of prejudices and fears, of uncertainties, and of all that
'infinite variety' which is the glory of our human nature. His love
poems run through almost the entire gamut of human emotions from
despair to ecstasy, and are evidence of an intimate knowledge of the
ways of the human heart which reminds one of Shakespeare.

Intolerant—as we have already seen—of the conventional stock
characters of Elizabethan love poetry—the languishing lover and the
sighing maiden, with their posturing and their stereotyped vocabulary
drained of all sensibility—Donne sought to rescue human love, and to
restore it where it belonged in the normal human milieu, where men
were neither beasts nor angels, but a mixture of both. In the early
Satyres and Elegies, to which reference was made in Chapter II, Donne
was sometimes guilty of the extreme of cynicism, and of seemingly
gross sensuality, in revolt against the old convention. But, as Grierson
so shrewdly remarks,[1] there is a world of difference between the witty
and passionate audacities of the young Donne, impatient of shams, of
the unreal, and the heartless sensuality of the Roman poet, Ovid, on
whose poems many of Donne's early attempts are modelled. For
Donne can very seldom be indifferent or detached in his poems. If he
shocks, he does so with intent, to shake us out of our lethargy to an
awareness of the real values, the real passions and tensions of the human
situation. And always, even in the most outrageous of the Elegies, e.g.
Variety and *Loves Progresse*, the extreme of the realism is redeemed by
the scintillating wit, the fun of the topsy-turvy logic which Donne
so often employs in his dialectic. The grossness of *The Anagram*, for
instance, is forgotten in our delight in the sparkling wit, while the
fallaciousness of its logic escapes us in the 'quick-fire' sequence of its

---

[1] H. J. C. Grierson, *The Poems of J. Donne*, Vol. II, 1912, Intro.

compressed syllogisms. Leishman draws our attention to the 'fallacy of the undistributed middle' in the argument contained in these lines:[2]

> All love is wonder; if we justly doe
> Account her wonderfull, why not lovely too?

But we must take care when marking the sophisms, not to miss the serious wit hidden in the ambiguous meaning Donne attaches to the word 'wonder'. Beneath the 'lyric grace', beneath the subtle play of the dialectic, there is the 'tough reasonableness' and the deeply-felt seriousness of the fact that, indeed, all love is wonder. This deep assurance about ultimate values is never very far from the nimble and often impish play of Donne's wit. Throughout the Elegies it is the vigour of the intellect working through the subtle dialectic which modifies the coarseness, distilling it to its essential terms, making it acceptable in a logical and very real sense.

Before we go on to examine Donne's treatment of the subject of human love in the *Songs and Sonets*—the most important body of his work—we will investigate, briefly, what were his views on man's soul and body and their relationship with each other, particularly in the profoundly intimate relationship of human love.

Donne, as we have seen in Chapter II, was fundamentally medieval in his ideas on man and his place in the scheme of things. As Miss Ramsay, the medieval scholar remarks:

> La tournure de sa pensée, le but de ses speculations, la forme sous laquelle cette pensée s'exprime, tout cela est essentiallement médiéval . . . La philosophie scholastique après tout est moins un systeme spécial q'une méthode de penser . . .[3]

To Donne, as to the scholastics who preceded him, and to the great minds who influenced him: Aristotle, Augustine and Aquinas, man was a composite being, uniting in himself the three souls, vegetative, sensitive and rational, this latter being regarded as man's highest faculty, that through which he came to the knowledge of ultimate Truth, and in the exercise of which he would be engaged throughout the length of the Beatific Vision.[4]

---

[2] J. B. Leishman, *The Monarch of Wit*, 1951, p. 74.
[3] M. P. Ramsay, *Les Doctrines Médiévales chez Donne*, 1924, p. 261.
[4] St. Thomas Aquinas tells us that: 'The prime author and mover of the universe

Catholic theology, in which Donne was trained from his earliest years, and in which he found the answers to his endless questions, was based upon the great synthesis built by St. Thomas Aquinas on the philosophy of Aristotle, incorporating the whole of Sacred Scripture and the works of the Fathers, particularly St. Augustine. While St. Thomas's attraction was to a study of the reality without us, St. Augustine, basing his theology on the philosophy of Plato, gave greater stress to the spiritual factors in life, with the aim of counteracting, to some extent, the decadence of life prevalent in the Roman Empire of his day. Though Donne was profoundly influenced by Augustine because of the affinity he felt with him, not only in the passionate directness of *The Confessions*, but in his Manichean traits which answered to the dualism of his own nature, yet I think it was St. Thomas, so eminently realist, who had the stronger attraction for his intellect.

In his *Essays in Divinity*, written 1614–15, Donne places St. Thomas beside St. Augustine, calling him, as he speaks to God in prayer

> another instrument and engine of Thine, whom Thou hadst so enabled that nothing was too mineral nor centric for the search and reach of his wit.[5]

This could perhaps be taken for Donne's free translation of the fundamental axiom of Thomistic psychology: 'Nihil est in intellectu quod non prius in sensu'—an axiom which must have appealed very strongly to our poet who spent so much of his energy trying to unravel

---

is intelligence . . . therefore the last end of the universe must be the good of the intelligence, and that is truth . . .'
Summa Contra Gentiles, trans. J. Rickaby, 1905, Bk I, Chap. I.
AND: 'Now the object of the intellect is the essence of a thing: hence the intellect attains to perfection so far as it knows the essence of what is before it. And therefore, when a man knows an effect, and knows that it has a cause, there is in him an outstanding natural desire of knowing the essence of the cause. If therefore, a human intellect knows the essence of a created effect without knowing aught of God beyond the fact of His existence, the perfection of that intellect does not yet adequately reach the First Cause, but the intellect has an outstanding natural desire of searching into the said Cause: hence it is not yet perfectly happy. For perfect happiness, therefore, it is necessary that the intellect shall reach as far as the very essence of the First Cause. (I–II, Q. III. Art. VIII).
Aquinas Ethicus, trans. J. Rickaby, Vol. I, p. 24, 1896.
[5] *Essays in Divinity*, 1651, p. 27.

the mystery of the 'subtile knot' linking the senses with the intelligence, the body with the soul.

St. Thomas was a true Aristotelian in basing his natural philosophy on the study of sensible objects, and in applying to them an appropriate, though dispassionate dialectic. Fr. Gilby tells us that in him

> emotion becomes tranquil through intelligence. With no sense of shock he illustrates the natural law, the image of God, and the divine perfections, from the humblest animal operations . . .

These, and the following lines, could have been written of Donne, and perfectly illustrate the affinity between them:

> Few thinkers are so continuist in joining everything to everything else . . . Reasoning is to understanding what time is to eternity, more a mind-in-the-making than a mind achieved . . . engaged in an environment discovered in bits and pieces, not yet enjoying the simple vision of everything in all . . .[6]

This is the man from whom Donne could have got confirmation of the fact that the mind is part of reality, that concepts denote sympathies, that thought itself is a passion—'passiones animae'—and that knower and known become one. But St. Thomas, the 'impenitent materialist', is also the great apologist for the body. He saw that in the mystery that is creation, flesh cannot be divorced from spirit, matter from form, soul from body. Compare this quotation from St. Thomas:

> Since . . . neither soul alone, nor body alone is man, but the thing called man arises out of their union, when God called man to the resurrection and the life, He called no mere part of man but the whole man, body and soul together in one,[7]

with this from a sermon preached by Donne at Whitehall, in 1628:

> . . . as God married thy body and soule together in the Creation, and shall at last crowne thy body and soule together in the Resurrection, so they may also rest together here . . .;[8]

or again, in his XXVI sermon:

> . . . the union of the soul and the body, by those spirits through

---

[6] T. Gilby, *Barbara Celarent*, 1949, p. 184.

[7] *De Resurrectione*, VIII, quoted by Etienne Gilson in *The Spirit of Medieval Philosophy*, 1950, p. 171.

[8] *Poetry & Prose*, Hayward, op. cit., p. 635.

which the soul exercises her faculties in the organs of the body, make up the man . . .[9]

There is no doubt that Donne fully accepted the doctrines of Catholic theology—in which he was so widely read—particularly concerning the nature of man's being. But there was that in his own nature which always prevented him from realizing the possibility of a harmonious functioning of body and soul, in this present life.

'Our life is a warfare, our whole life', he grimly asserts.[10]

It is possible that his attachment to both these Fathers, the Platonic Augustine and the Aristotelian Thomas, is another evidence of the tension within his being: the desire of his ardent spirit for transcendental joys being continually thwarted by the equally strong desire of his body for sensual satisfaction. As a poet his business was not however the making of a synthesis, but the portraying in convincing form of the struggle in the heart of man towards a wholeness and a harmony, always beyond his reach, but attainable, momentarily, in rare moments of ecstasy or of insight. We should therefore expect to find a very real ambivalence in the poetry of Donne—now making an extreme plea for the rights of the body in the justification of natural love, as is his aim in *Loves Progress*, and at another time defending the rôle of the spirit, or soul, in human love, in such poems as *The Extasie* where he declares concerning the lovers' bodies:

They are ours, though they are not wee . . .

This ambivalence is at the root of the tension which gives to Donne's greatest poetry the character of a living experience, when we feel, like Lear, in the presence of 'the thing itself'.

More usually, however, we find Donne baffled, unable to come to terms with the war between flesh and spirit. In *Loves Alchymie*, we find him posing the two extremes: love as mere lust, and love which is the marriage of true minds, as adversaries in a disputation, each defeating the other:

Ends love in this, that my man,
Can be as happy' as I can; If he can
Endure the short scorne of a Bridegroomes play?
That loving wretch that sweares,
'Tis not the bodies marry, but the mindes,

---

[9] Quoted by Mrs. Bennett, in 'The Love Poetry of J. Donne': *17th Century Studies Presented to Sir H. Grierson*, 1938, p. 95.
[10] *Poetry & Prose*, Hayward, op. cit., p. 665.

> Which he in her Angelique findes,
> Would sweare as justly, that he heares,
> In that dayes rude hoarse minstralsey, the spheares.

No compromise is offered, no logical truce concluded. The final couplet:

> Hope not for minde in women; at their best
> Sweetnesse and wit, they're but Mummy, possest.

merely asserts the impossibility of satisfaction in either extreme, and we are left with nothing but the fleeting, ambiguous comfort of

> . . . a winter—seeming summers night.

In *Negative Love*, we have an adaptation of the dialectic of negation, so frequent in the scholastic method and so masterly employed by St. Thomas, here used by Donne to analyse his own response to love. Though he declares he is attracted neither by the physical 'eye, cheeke, lip', nor by the spiritual 'vertue of the minde', he yet is unable to say positively what it is that inflames his love:

> If that be simply perfectest
> Which can by no way be exprest
> But Negatives, my love is so . . .

Helen Gardner makes the remark that

> Donne was a man of strong passions, in whom an appetite for life was crossed by a deep distaste for it.[11]

While I agree with the first part of this statement, I should prefer to think that Donne's appetite for life was crossed, not by a distaste for it, but by a realization of its innate futility—a realization that full satisfaction for one's whole being, body and soul, could be attained only by union with ultimate Reality, ultimate Essence and Truth, through the exercise of the intelligence . . .

> For perfect happiness . . . it is necessary that the intellect shall reach as far as the very essence of the First Cause. (see Footnote 4).

---

[11] H. Gardner, *The Divine Poems*, 1952, Intro., p. xxxv.

THEME OF THE INTERDEPENDENCE OF SOUL AND BODY

In my opinion, Donne's best love poems—in which his personal voice is most clearly heard—are those in which he explores by means of a skilful dialectic and rare imagery, the subtle reality of the interdependence of soul and body, that mysterious and ineffable metaphysical balance which is at the heart of perfect love.

Such a poem is *Aire and Angels*. While acknowledged as one of Donne's most beautiful lyrics it has however been very much misunderstood. Helen Gardner considers that on the whole it is not a successful poem, because of the unease she feels in interpreting it as based on the conception of male initiative, and of men and women as unequal partners in the creation of love.[12] I am not happy with this interpretation of the poem, and feel that Alvarez is much nearer the truth when he declares the subject of the poem to be concerned with the progress of love, from the ideal to the overwhelmingly physical, and back, finally, to a delicate harmony between the two.[13]

In *Aire and Angels* Donne is investigating the rôles which matter and spirit—or body and soul—play in human love. The opening of the poem, contrasting vividly with Donne's usually boisterous manner, suggests the tender awakening of love, and introduces the Angel image on which the whole meaning of the poem turns:

> Twice or thrice had I loved thee,
> Before I knew thy face or name;
> So in a voice, so in a shapeless flame,
> Angels affect us oft, and worship'd bee.

He then explores, dialectically, the development of love from its spiritual, and altogether angelic beginnings, to its inevitable capitulation to the physical details of 'lip, eye, and brow', and he decides, that since human love cannot express itself if it be wholly of the spirit, nor survive if it become merely carnal and sensual, for

> Ev'ry thy haire for love to worke upon
> Is much too much, some fitter must be sought;
> For, not in nothing, nor in things
> Extreme, and scatt'ring bright, can love inhere . . .

---

[12] H. Gardner, 'Interpretation of Aire and Angels' in *The Business of Criticism*, 1959, pp. 62–75.

[13] A. Alvarez, *The School of Donne*, 1961, Chap. I.

then the only way to preserve it is by means of a subtle surrender—a rarefied balance—that takes account of both elements. It is seldom that Donne can portray the tension within himself in lines of such human poignancy. Consistently logical and dialectically searching, as always, he illustrates his point by the wonderfully apt image of the angel giving expression to its spiritual essence, through the medium of air, the purest of material substances:[14]

> Then as an Angell, face, and wings
> Of aire, not pure as it, yet pure doth weare,
> So thy love may be my loves spheare . . .

The misunderstandings concerning the poem have arisen chiefly in connection with the interpretation of the three final lines:

> Just such disparitie
> As is twixt Aire and Angells puritie,
> 'Twixt womens love, and mens will ever bee.

Dr. Leavis comments on its 'blandly insolent matter-of-factness';[15] Crofts considers it a 'quiet insult' to womankind;[16] while Unger sees in it a mere witty reversal with ironic overtones.[17] Helen Gardner is right in maintaining that this last interpretation of Unger's would make the whole poem 'artistically trivial'. I should like to quote here a passage from one of Donne's sermons to which she draws our attention:

> The force of the whole piece is for the most part left to the shutting up; the whole frame of the poem is a beating out of a piece of gold, but the last clause is as the impression of the stamp, and that is it that makes it current.[18]

It is not likely therefore, that in a poem of such seriousness and of such

---

[14] 'Et sic Angeli assumunt corpora ex aera, condensando ipsum virtute divina, quantam necesse est ad corporis assumendi formationem . . .' (from St. Thomas's teaching on the nature of Angels, quoted by Mrs. Bennett in *Seventeenth Century Studies presented to H. Grierson*, op. cit., p. 99).

[15] F. R. Leavis, *Revaluation*, 1936, p. 12.

[16] J. E. V. Crofts, 'J. Donne: A Reconsideration' in *Twentieth Century Views*, ed. H. Gardner, 1962.

[17] L. Unger, *Donne's Poetry & Modern Criticism*, Chicago, 1950, p. 44.

[18] H. Gardner, *The Metaphysical Poets*, Intro., p. 21.

superb craftsmanship, Donne could find no better ending than in a gibe against women, however much—as some claim—he may have been supported by traditional teaching on the subject.[19]

Donne is certainly making an important point in these final lines—in fact it is the central point of the entire poem—and I think that our interpretation must hinge upon the meaning he attaches to the vital phrase: 'Just such disparitie'. Far from being a sudden reversal or a mocking taunt, these lines make a splendid 'shutting up' for the entire poem, and refer, not to the disparity between the active and passive qualities respectively of the love of men and women, but to the metaphysical disparity between the spiritual and material elements present in all human love. Donne is saying, in effect, that, just as an Angel is invisible, is incapable of expressing its beauty in human terms without the help of air—'not pure as it'—so all human love, spiritual also in its origin, is 'deed-bound', incapable of communicating itself to its loved one, without the help of the body which is, in physical fact, 'loves spheare'.

Because *Aire and Angels* is a poem concerned more with the ideal than the real, we do not feel that Donne is here as emotionally involved as he is, for instance, in *The Extasie*. The gently lyric opening, the carefully balanced structure and the musical flow of the verse are evidence of the fact—rare in the poetry of Donne—that here his intelligence is engaged rather than his heart. He is writing about the ideal interdependence of soul and body, an ideal for which his whole being longed, but which his turbulent nature could never attain. Hence the dispassionate dialectic, the purpose of which is the balancing of 'loves pinnace', while at the same time it justifies and explores the ideal ministry of matter in the service of the spirit, or the ideal function of the body in the expression of human love.

The Extasie: Another poem on this subject of the metaphysical relationship between soul and body is *The Extasie*, concerning which even a greater controversy waged among critics.

Coleridge praises it, saying he should never find fault with metaphysical poems if they were even half as excellent as this;[20] Legouis

---

[19] B. Keckermann, *Systema Systematum*, 1013, p. 573:
'Aristotle had said: "For females are weaker and colder in nature, and we must look upon the female character as being a sort of a natural deficiency" ' from Aristotle's treatise on Natural science, IV. 6. 775a (quoted by W. T. Costello in *The Scholastic Curriculum, 17th Century Cambridge*).
[20] *Coleridge's Miscellaneous Criticism*, ed. T. M. Raysor, 1936, p. 138.

sees it as a piece of clever seduction where Donne stands 'self-revealed in his hypocritical game'[21]; Grierson, whose views are supported by Helen Gardner, Mrs. Bennett and other eminent scholars, sees the poem mainly as an impassioned argument for the 'interdependence of the soul and body'[22]; while Professor G. R. Potter regards it as a highly serious attempt to find the answer to the riddle of man's personality.[23]

Once again, with perhaps a more precise dialectic, Donne's spirit wanders out into that mysterious borderland between matter and spirit, where ecstasies take place, and from that unexplored 'no-man's-land' he brings us, in the detached tones of dialectic, the ineffable, 'unperplexed'.

The title is significant, and, as is usual with Donne's titles, represents the highly compressed proposition of a thesis he is about to investigate. Ecstasy occurs at the height of passion, and means being outside the self—'I live, now not I': the losing of self in the infinity of another. It is from this height of exaltation that Donne seeks to penetrate the mystery of oneness in love.

It is interesting to note the differing conceptions there are about the nature of ecstasy. Helen Gardner is of the opinion that it is a state of blissful quiet, and she therefore contends that since the minds of the lovers are 'active as fleas' the tone of the poem is incompatible with its subject. But Miss Ramsay points out, that according to the accounts which St. Teresa of Avila gives of her ecstasies, they were in fact violent and energetic states. The traditional teaching of the Church on the subject of ecstasies (see *Western Mysticism* by Cuthbert Butler) is that in the contemplative or ecstatic state there is intense activity at the highest level of intelligence, and it is against this traditional background that Donne composed his *Extasie*. It is likely too—as some students of Donne have pointed out—that he had read the classics of the Spanish mystics, St. John of the Cross and St. Teresa.

Helen Gardner in an illuminating article[24] discusses the common ground on which the dispute about the poem's meaning has arisen: that the lovers should turn from the enjoyment of spiritual communion to the pleasures of the physical. Both sides, she remarks, take it for granted that the theme of the poem is a justification of physical love as compatible with the highest form of ideal love, and that the dispute

---

[21] P. Legouis, *Donne the Craftsman*, 1928, p. 69.

[22] H. J. C. Grierson, *The Poems of J. Donne*, 1912, Vol. II. Intro.

[23] 'Donne's Extasie, Contra Legouis', *P.Q.*, XV, No. 3, 1936.

[24] H. Gardner, 'The Argument about The Extasie' in *Elizabethan and Jacobean Studies presented to F. P. Wilson*, 1959.

hinges on whether this justification is seriously meant, or whether it is merely a sophisticated piece of seduction.

Her own position is rather unusual, combining elements from both views. While she regards the poem as wholly serious in intention, she does not consider that the argument fully justifies the body's claim in love. She gives a very interesting and full account of Leone Ebreo's description of the semi-death of ecstasy, from his '*Dialoghi d'Amore*'[25] written ca. 1502, which she considers as the literary source for Donne's Extasie.

Her interpretation of the poem from line 49—

> But O alas, so long, so farre . . .

is based on Ebreo's idea of ecstasy: that its force could be so strong that it might break the bond between soul and body, and lead to the death of rapture. It is from this death in ecstasy, H. Gardner claims, that the lovers withdraw, to return to the ordinary life in the body, so that the union argued for in the concluding verses is not, according to her, the union of the lovers with each other, but the re-union of each soul with its own body. The concern of the lovers is that the bond of the new, 'abler soul' will still subsist 'when we' are to bodies gone'.

A. J. Smith[26] who also traces *The Extasie* from Ebreo, arrives at some different conclusions. Quoting from the *Dialoghi*—

> with the correspondence of the bodily union, the spiritual love is augmented and made more perfect . . .

he concludes that the argument at the end of the poem does refer to the union of the lovers with each other, and moreover, that this resorting to their bodies will mean no debasing of their love, nor shortening of their eternal union.

Though both Helen Gardner's and A. J. Smith's scholarly researches have helped to make the poem more intelligible, more consonant with our knowledge of Donne, the scholar, yet, in my opinion, Grierson's

---

[25] This was an ambitious attempt to synthesise all the intellectual traditions of Europe, and was one of the main sources of 16th century Platonism. Resemblances are traced between Ebreo's work and such topics from Donne's poem, as, that sight is emitted from the eye by means of rays; the 'compounded' nature of the soul; and the gold-alloy metaphor for the relationship of soul and body.

[26] A. J. Smith, 'The Metaphysic of love', *RES*, Nov. 1958.

earlier interpretation stands to-day as the classic and orthodox view
of the poem:

> Here, with the same intensity of feeling (as in *The Nocturnall*), and
> in the same abstract dialectical erudite strain, he emphasizes the
> interdependence of soul and body . . .[27]

He is of the opinion, however, that Donne is not altogether successful
in his aim; that he appears to fall into that dualism which he is trying
to transcend . . .

> They are ours, though they are not wee . . .

and so arrives at no final resolution of the problem. But could there be
a final resolution for Donne? I must confess that, for me, the whole
attraction of the poem lies in the fact that here Donne is being truly and
characteristically himself: the man torn between earth and heaven, his
spirit soaring into ecstasy, his intellect searching sublime suprasensory
regions, while his human heart and body hunger for the delights of
sense, the eternity of lovers' hours.

While in *Aire and Angels*, Donne is concerned to prove that the parity
and perfection of love depend upon the achieving of a delicate balance
between its spiritual and its physical constituents—demonstrating the
ideal, in fact—in *The Extasie* he is more truly and more typically concerned with demonstrating the real. Here we do not find the tenuous
imaginative balance of *Aire and Angels*, but the sombre fact of the
imbalance of our human state, and the resultant difficulty in reconciling
the mysterious elements which make us man.

In my opinion, it is as misleading to declare that *The Extasie* is a poem
justifying either the physical or the spiritual elements in human love,
as it is to say it is a poem of seduction. For, above and beyond all else,
it is a poem about two persons in love; not two bodies nor two souls,
but two people each of whom is a 'body-mind', constituting that
wonderful and mysterious infinity of the human person.

Donne, with his probing, scientific mind, thinks that the best way to
understand the mystery is to separate the constituent parts, examine
them under the white light of his dialectic method, and then perhaps
discover the secret that

> makes both one, each this and that.

---

[27] *The Poems of J. Donne*, 1912, Vol. II, Intro.

Immediately we see the aptness of his title—ecstasy—meaning a temporary separation of soul from body, not in the sense of trance, but in the sense of the highly active contemplation of the Teresian ecstasy, where the things of sense are viewed in their proper perspective, and correct standards of value are re-established, so that the 'unperplexed' soul can return to put its normal existence into order. The Persian poem in Bremond's *Prayer and Poetry* (see Appendix A) comes nearest to the meaning of *The Extasie*, telling as it does of the lover returning from the desert with new insight, new awareness, and so more worthy of the Beloved.

Helen Gardner is correct in stating that too long a rapture would bring death to the body, and that therefore the souls of the lovers must now resume possession of their bodies, but there is a danger that she is omitting part of the truth when she interprets

Else a great Prince in prison lies

as the soul of each lover animating his own body only, pointing out that here Donne is contrasting the Platonic view of the soul as imprisoned in the flesh, with the Aristotelian (and Thomistic) conception of the union of soul and body in man. I feel certain that Donne meant very much more than that.

The first fact established during the course of the ecstasy is that love, which

interinanimates two souls

produces an 'abler soule' or 'new soule' 'whom no change can invade'. It is this new soul, joining the 'thou' and the 'I', which returns to animate the bodies of the lovers, to reproduce in them the 'interinanimation' already experienced in the extrasensory region of the ecstasy:

Soe soule into the soule may flow
Though it to body first repaire.

In these final verses I think that Donne is not so much justifying the physical side of love, as endeavouring to express an ineffable experience, in the same dispassionate dialectic he had used in recounting the ecstasy. His failure to unravel the 'subtile knot' where two infinities meet in one; to find in physical terms an equation for the 'dialogue of one', is a guarantee of the honesty of Donne's thought, which, however

9

daring, however keen, would need more than a metaphysician's insight and a more than human detachment to portray ecstasy incarnate.

Donne does analyse for us, in the clear, penetrating light of *The Extasie*, the birth and growth of love in human hearts, from the physical details of the senses, which

> Did us, to us, at first convay,

to the sublime 'interinanimation' which makes two souls one in spiritual rapture. And we must remember that this is precisely what the poem is about—spiritual rapture. When critics complain about the laboured plod of the lines which follow:

> To our bodies turne wee then, that so
> Weake men on love reveal'd may looke:
> Loves mysteries in soules do grow,
> But yet the body is his booke,

it may be because they are following their own line of reasoning, not Donne's. May he not well have meant to portray poetically how flat the post-ecstatic period could be?—how laboursome the descent from Thabor? Always the realist, Donne is writing about life and love *as they are*. He knows that our moments of ecstasy are granted us but to clear our vision, to

> unperplex . . . and tell us what we love . . .

so that our acts, the normal, everyday give-and-take of love may not be soul-less, but rather the true expression of the inmost spiritual core of our being—

> Else a great Prince in prison lies.

C. S. Lewis remarks that the longing for perfect union in love, made forever unattainable by our mutually excluding bodies, can have the grandeur of a metaphysical pursuit.[28] In *The Extasie*, it has also the strain of such a pursuit. We feel it in the cautious, slow-moving verses of the introduction:

> Our soules, (which to advance their state,
> Were gone out,) hung'twixt her, and mee.

---

[28] *The Four Loves*, 1960, p. 94.

And whil'st our soules negotiate there,
Wee like sepulchrall statues lay . . .;

in the more halting dialectic; and in the abrupt staccato pattern of the
rhythm. There is nothing facile or artificial here; nothing of the shining
ideal which lent such lyric grace to *Aire and Angels*. Instead, we are
conscious in every verse of the passionate seriousness and the earnest
intellectual striving of Donne, to prove that spiritual ecstasy does not
exclude, but rather gives meaning to the physical ecstasy, and that
in the truest human love they are one:

And if some lover, such as wee,
Have heard this dialogue of one,
Let him still marke us, he shall see
Small change, when we' are to bodies gone.

THEME OF MUTUAL LOVE

We now come to the poems which celebrate the theme of mutual love, and in these we come closest, perhaps, to the identification of the ideal and the real, art and experience, in the poetry of Donne. Not that any of these poems can be directly connected with actual events in Donne's life, with the exception of the *Valediction: forbidding Mourning* which, as we have seen, was written for his wife on the eve of his departure for France with Sir Robert Drury, in 1611. But though they cannot be regarded as autobiographical; though these poems should be judged, a priori, as works of art; and though we have Donne's word denying their value as records of personal experience:

> I did best when I had least truth for my subject,[29]

we cannot altogether deny the influence of a poet's experiences on his intellectual life, and on the measure and kind of his emotional response to situations, or to inspirations. The mutual-love theme celebrated in the poems we are about to discuss was, at one and the same time, the ideal fulfilment and security Donne sought amidst the changing flux of life, and evidence of the reality he experienced in his love for Ann More. There is therefore less tension, less ambiguity, less straining of the dialectic after a delicate metaphysical balance, in these poems, than for instance, in *The Extasie*.

In the *Good Morrow*, Donne adapts with exquisite tact, the literary type of the aubade—a song of lovers awakening at dawn—to symbolize the awakening of the lovers to a new kind of life, the glories of which are heightened by contrast, not only with the sensual past when they were

> suck'd on countrey pleasures, childishly,

but with the more mature and progressive present, where men venture forth in search of a better life in 'new worlds', while they in the 'one little roome' of their love are, in fact, all the world to each other:

> Let us possesse one world, each hath one, and is one.

---

[29] Quoted by H. J. C. Grierson in *Cambridge Hist. Eng. Literature*, 1909, Vol. IV, Chap. XI.

THE DIALECTIC IN THE LOVE POEMS

What constantly amazes one about Donne is that the greater the passion and the tenderness, the more precise is the logic, and the more intricate the thought. One is reminded of Coleridge's definition of the imagination which he declares reveals itself in a balance of discordant qualities, such as sameness with difference, and a more than usual state of emotion with more than usual order. In this poem celebrating perfect love, Donne employs the significant metaphor of the spiritual microcosm to signify the eternal, unchanging equality of their love—

> Where can we finde two better hemispheares . . .

contrasting it with the material macrocosm which is subject to the change and decay implied in the phrases 'sharpe Northe' and 'declining West'. In the final lines he argues, wittily and fallaciously (as we have seen on p. 82), from the physical world he has disdained, to stress once again the qualities which give permanence to their love:

> If our two loves be one, or, thou and I
> Love so alike, that none doe slacken, none can die.

We are reminded of De Quincey's remark in his Essay on Pope, that poetry

> can teach only as nature teaches, as forests teach, as the sea teaches
> . . . by deep impulse, by hieroglyphic suggestion.

Note how the casual conversational tempo of the opening is quickened by the repetitive questioning, only to be arrested by the sudden dramatic pause after the emphatic spondee: 'T'was so':

> I wonder by my troth, what thou, and I
> Did, till we lov'd? were we not wean'd till then?
> But suck'd on countrey pleasures, childishly?
> Or snorted we in the seven sleepers den?
> T'was so.

It is as if Donne himself were struck by the sudden revelation of the wonderful truth conveyed by the lines which follow:

> But this, all pleasures fancies bee.
> If ever any beauty I did see,
> Which I desir'd, and got, t'was but a dreame of thee.

We note also how he can make use of the homeliest image and the most transparent language to express his sublime ideal of this mutual, trusting love:

> My face in thine eye, thine in mine appeares,
> And true plaine hearts doe in the faces rest . . .

In *The Good Morrow* one must marvel at the way Donne's dialectic curls with the ebb and flow of his passion, using the most abstruse argument as well as the everyday idiom to convey its exact quality. This is indeed the 'masculine line' so much admired by Donne's contemporaries, but criticised by Dryden who accused him of perplexing the 'minds of the fair sex with nice speculations of philosophy, when he should engage their hearts, and entertain them with the softnesses of love.' But when one reflects one must realise that the virile strength and intellectual challenge of Donne's love poems are a far greater compliment to woman than the sentimental songs and serenades, with their outworn imagery and stale flattery.

Donne woos the intelligence rather than the heart, sometimes employing shock tactics that to Dryden would certainly sound most unloverlike—as in the dramatic opening of *A Lecture Upon the Shadow*:

> Stand still, and I will read to thee
> A Lecture, love, In Loves philosophy.

His emotion is wonderfully controlled by the rhythmic logic with which he then proceeds to trace the analogy between the vanquishing of shadows by the sun as it attains full noon, and the gradual overcoming of doubts and fears by love, as it develops into a perfect, mutual trust:

> That love hath not attain'd the high'st degree,
> Which is still diligent lest others see.

In the second stanza, as if carried away by the argument, or as if the logician had for the time being ousted the lover, Donne relates the lengthening shadows cast by the sun in the afternoon and evening to the deceptions and the unfaithfulness which attend the decline of love:

> The morning shadowes weare away
> But these grow longer all the day.

In the last line of the stanza, however, the lover quite literally 'butts' in with

> But oh, loves day is short, if love decay.

In the couplet which completes this poem we hear again the authentic voice of Donne the supreme realist, who will never yield to logical consistency when it conflicts with the truth of his experience. The analogy between true love and the sun holds good, he seems to say, only until both have reached their noon:

> Love is a growing, or full constant light;
> And his first minute, after noone, is night.

There is a grim finality about this couplet, an uncompromising directness which startles while it convinces, and yet flatters while it demands the all of love with the boldness of a lover.

The Sunne Rising: In the *Sunne Rising*, in a style very different from either of the poems we have just examined, Donne once more treats of the all-sufficiency of the two lovers. An impudent wit replaces the grave tenderness of *The Good Morrow*, as the lover turns aside to chide the intruding world:

> Busie old foole, unruly Sunne . . .
> Sawcy pedantique wretch, goe chide
> Late schoole boyes and sowre prentices,
> Goe tell Court-huntsmen, that the King will ride,
> Call countrey ants to harvest offices . . .

A more subtly complicated dialectic contrasts with the controlled logic of *A Lecture Upon the Shadow*, as we travel in the wake of the Sun, surveying the spiced and splendid Continents of the Orient with their gorgeous courts and Capitals, only to conclude, in the climactic line of the poem, that in comparison with love they are all but unreal, unsubstantial shadows—

> Nothing else is—

for

> She is all States, and all Princes, I . . .
> Princes doe but play us; compar'd to this,
> All honor's mimique; All wealth alchimie . . .

Here, though he seems to 'daff the world aside' for love:

> Love, all alike, no season knowes, nor clyme,
> Nor houres, dayes, moneths, which are the rags of time,

Donne sees his love not so much renouncing the world as epitomizing it, giving meaning to its honour, beauty and wealth. The idea that this 'contracted' world of the lovers, this world of mutual, satisfying love, is the only reality, is the higher truth emphasized by the logical fallacies which occur in the final lines:

> Thine age askes ease, and since thy duties bee
> To warme the world, that's done in warming us.
> Shine here to us, and thou art every where;
> This bed thy center is, these walls, thy spheare.

Here perhaps, as also in *The Canonization*, there is for Donne more than a casual backward glance; it may well be that he 'doth protest too much' in his deriding of 'Court-huntsmen' and 'countrey ants'. No detachment can be so complete as not to admit the odd wistful backward look at the things one has sacrificed . . .

> What heart can be so sure of itself as to guarantee that no feeling of regret will slip between resignation, which depends upon ourselves, and forgetfulness which can only come with time?
>
>   *Eugène Fromentin.*

We have found that Donne's persistent aim was to search for the truth by dialectical means, and it may be that in these instances, in the grip of strong emotion, he said more than he knew.

The Anniversarie: The last poem on this theme to which I shall refer, is the most moving expression of Donne's conception of mutual love as an eternal, abiding reality. I do not know any critic who has written so well of it as Grierson, who speaks of the quickening of the brain, the passion gathering sweep, the clearer consciousness perceiving the eternal significance of love, . . .

'to me', he adds, 'it seems that the joy of love has never been expressed at once with such intensity and such elevation'.[30]

The dialectic is there, of course, as always; the weaving back and forth of the web of argument—not now to 'dispute and conquer', not to discover the happy via media, nor yet to explore the metaphysical frontiers where body and soul meet and are fused in the ecstasy of perfect love, but here to give utterance to profound and moving realities: that while the Sun, and

> All other things, to their destruction draw,
> Only our love hath no decay;
> This, no to-morrow hath, nor yesterday,
> Running, it never runs from us away,
> But truly keepes his first, last, everlasting day.

Here, there is no urgent 'carpe diem' cry, no pining in the sombre reflection that

> wee
> Must leave at last in death, these eyes, and eares.

The grave holds no fears for a faith that looks through death, for

> then wee shall be thoroughly blest . . .;

nor can it shake the assurance of these lines, where the living passion pulses through the ordered measures of verse:

> True and false feares let us refraine,
> Let us live nobly, and live, and add againe
> Yeares and yeares unto yeares . . .

Grierson has remarked that there is nothing quite like Donne's love poetry—in its expression of fullness of joy in contented love—in the language, except perhaps some of Browning's, and that no love poetry of the period has more of the beat of real feeling in it except Shakespeare's. Donne does indeed almost formulate a new philosophy of love: less transcendental than Dante, more passionate than the Roman

[30] H. J. C. Grierson, The Poems of J. Donne, 1912, Vol. II, Intro.

lyrists, less ascetic than the medieval poets, more really spiritual than Petrarch because he is more true to the human situation and to the facts of human love. He is concerned not to write about love as 'the coral lips and Cupid's golden wings and the opening rose' which C. S. Lewis seems to prefer;[31] not to tell us what his mistress is like; not to indulge in the pagan cry that time would stay its course, which we can hear in Marvell's *Coy Mistress*, and in so much of Herrick. He is concerned to say only what it is like to be a human being in love with another human being: two persons of diverse moods, two worlds encompassing love's infinite variety, two infinities that yet are one in the ineffably sweet mystery of human love.

It was through this experience of mutual love that Donne felt himself in contact with metaphysical reality, a reality that took account of the different realms of being, and that answered to his inmost need. For Donne, as for Lear at the end, nothing else was. His attachment to the symbol of the microcosm is significant of his desire for security; for the ordered, inclusive world of love at the still point of the turning sphere which was his life. But neither Donne the man of turbulent passion, nor the poet forever seeking truth by means of his keen-edged dialectic, could find his soul's rest in a security or a love which, after all, were but figures of ultimate Reality, transcendent Truth and perfect Love.

Cleanth Brooks remarks that

> Donne's imagination seems obsessed with the problems of unity; the sense in which the lovers become one, the sense in which the soul is united with God.[32]

Donne did not wait to seek God until he had left the carnal for the spiritual; rather it was the spiritual element ever present in his human love, and so prominent in the poems we have been studying, that brought him at last to the top of the

'huge hill
Cragged and steep', where 'Truth stands'.

---

[31] C. S. Lewis, 'Donne and Love Poetry in 17th Century' in *Seventeenth Century Studies presented to Sir H. J. C. Grierson*, 1938, p. 81.
[32] *The Well Wrought Urn*, 1949, p. 17.

'For though through many streights, and lands I roame,
I launch at Paradise, and I saile towards home.'

The Progresse of the Soule

CHAPTER VI

THE DIALECTIC OF ULTIMATE REALITY IN THE *DIVINE POEMS*

DONNE'S work, in prose and in poetry—in the *Elegies* and in the *Songs and Sonets*, in the *Divine Poems*, and in the Sermons—was all of a piece. Though in many of the *Divine Poems* we miss the nervous tension, the complexity of attitudes, the straining dialectic, the living flux of life perceptible in the earlier poems, we still can hear the authentic voice of Donne, now rarely harsh or grating, but still searching in the same precise fashion for the One among the Many. His aim from the beginning was to analyse and lay bare, by means of an exacting dialectical method, his own moods and reflections in the experiences which meant most to him—the experiences in which his body and soul, his intellect as well as his 'cerebral muscles' were fully engaged, and which formed, as it were, a bridge between physical and metaphysical reality, the world of appearances and the world of the real. Even in his most cynical elegies, even while he railed and abused, he divined another relationship which transcended human limitations and partings, while in the most passionate of the *Songs and Sonets* he sought the permanence and the oneness which union with the source of all Love and Truth alone could give him. As Miss Ramsay so rightly comments:

> Toujours, et au fond de toute pensée, il y a chez lui le sentiment religieux. À tout moment cela se retrouve dans ses lettres, et il en est de même dans sa poésie . . .[1]

Donne had fought for many years against King James's expressed wish that he become a divine, and it was only with extreme reluctance, and perhaps because now in his forties he saw no other hope of preferment, he decided to take orders in the Anglican Church. He was ordained in January 1614/15, and soon afterwards appointed Reader in Divinity to the Benchers of Lincoln's Inn. The years 1619 and 1620 were spent in foreign travel, and on his return, in 1621, he was appointed Dean of

---

[1] M. P. Ramsay, *Les Doctrines Médiévales chez Donne*, 1924, p. 268

St. Paul's. Though students of Donne trace some of the *Divine Poems* and *Holy Sonnets* to the years following his ordination, his great gifts of mind and heart were from now on employed, primarily, in the preparation of his sermons.

> The latter part of his life may be said to be a continued study; for as he usually preached once a week, if not oftener, so after his Sermon he never gave his eyes rest, till he had chosen out a new Text, and that night cast his Sermon into a form, and his Text into divisions; and the next day betook himself to consult the Fathers, and so commit his meditations to his memory, which was excellent.[2]

The death of his wife, Ann, in 1617, was the occasion of the *Holy Sonnet XVII:*

> Since she whom I lov'd hath payd her last debt . . .

one of the most characteristic, and certainly, the most personal of the *Divine Poems.* Here we find Donne's intellectual conviction that, with his wife's death, God is now his all in all—

> Wholly on heavenly things my mind is sett—

being assailed in the very process of its shaping by the sensible cravings of his earth-bound nature, which he is too realistically honest to deny:

> A holy thirsty dropsy melts me yett . . .

Tillyard concludes that such contradictions within the logical structure of the poem betray an unusual cast of mind in Donne—

> a reluctance to reach conclusions, a keener relish for the processes than for the issues of thought . . .[3]

But, as has been demonstrated earlier, Donne is more interested in analysing and presenting the truth of his own experience, in portraying for us 'live thoughts in live brains', than in giving us neat conclusions,

---

[2] *Walton's Lives*, 'The Life of Dr. J. Donne', 1903, p. 62.
[3] E. M. W. Tillyard, *The Metaphysicals & Milton*, 1956, Intro., p. 5.

poetic 'Q.E.D.s', from which all the sensibility, all the contradiction, all the attractive inconsistencies of his nature would have been drained. In this poem I think he is being humble in the truest and finest sense, i.e., recognizing the limitations of his fallen nature, when he says to God in its closing lines:

> (Thou) dost not only feare least I allow
> My love to Saints and Angels things divine,
> But in thy tender jealosy dost doubt
> Least the World, Fleshe, yea Devill putt thee out.

The main point which he makes, however, lies in these terse lines:

> Here the admyring her my mind did whett
> To seeke thee God; so streames do shew their head . . .

Since all things drew Donne to their source and centre this is what we should expect—that his experience of human love should lead him to a greater realization of the source of all Love. His 'holy thirsty dropsy' will be satisfied only at the Fountainhead itself.

Increasingly through his life was ingrained in Donne's nature a deep sense of the vanity of all things earthly, a sense which was strengthened by the swiftness and frequency with which death struck both within his family and outside it—in the case of a young favourite such as Essex, or of a brilliant young scholar such as Edmund Campion. This text of 'vanitas vanitatem' was a frequent one in his sermons, later in life, as we read in one given in 1622:

> To know, that all the glory of man, is as the flower of grass: that even the glory, and all the glory of man, of all mankind, is but a flower . . . somewhat less than the proto-type, than the original, than the flower itself . . . To know how near nothing, how meer nothing, all the glory of this world is, is a good, a great degree of learning . . .[4]

Both *The First Anniversary* and *The Second Anniversary*, which for all their ungainly rambling, still do marvellously transcend their ostensible occasions, have as their theme this sense of the vanity and emptiness of

---

[4] *Poetry & Prose*, Hayward, p. 736.

all things here below. These poems, written in 1611 and 1612, at the request of Donne's patron, Sir Robert Drury, were the only poems published in his life-time. They form a bridge between his earlier secular poems and the bulk of his *Divine Poems*.

Martz calls *The Second Anniversary* one of the great religious poems of the seventeenth century. In order to demonstrate its careful crafts-manship he has analysed its total design thus: an introduction; followed by seven sections each comprising a meditation bearing on the subject matter of the poem and a eulogy of the dead girl; and a conclusion which takes up the last eighteen lines of the poem.[5] In so far as such an analysis helps us to grasp Donne's total design in the poem it is of great importance. Otherwise there is a danger that we will find the repetition of ideas within the sections tiresome, and the refrain in honour of Elizabeth Drury fulsome.

In this poem Donne views man and his life on earth from the per-spective of eternity. We are advised:

> . . . up unto the watch-towre get,
> And see all things despoyl'd of fallacies . . .

From this station Donne bids us look down upon the pitiful antics of man here below, but at the end of each section—or meditation—as if to correct our vision, he introduces the refrain, which has the double value of distracting us from our immediate preoccupation with our dismal earthly lot, and of forcing us to look above, to the life which lasts forever, and symbolized in this poem as in *The First Anniversary*, by the resurrected spirit of Elizabeth Drury. Thus having in the first section demonstrated that this world is 'but a carkasse', he cries:

> Look upward; that's towards her, whose happy state
> We now lament not, but congratulate.
> Shee, to whom all this world was but a stage,
> Where all sat harkning how her youthfull age
> Should be emploi'd, because in all shee did,
> Some Figure of the Golden times was hid . . .

The fallacies in which mortal men indulge are treated, not with the ruthless dialectic we have become accustomed to, but with a degree of kindly, and even humorous chiding, the temper we should expect

---

[5] *The Poetry of Meditation*, 1954, pp. 220-236.

of a man who was endeavouring now to see things 'sub specie aeternitatis'. Having gravely listed the gaps in man's meagre store of knowledge—

> Why grasse is greene, or why our blood is red . . .

he draws the logical conclusion:

> What hope have wee to know ourselves, when wee
> Know not the least things, which for our use be?

Donne goes on to ask the central question of the poem:

> . . . what essential joy can'st thou expect
> Here upon earth? What permanent effect
> Of transitory causes?

Then by means of the logical principle of 'comparison by the more or
less'—

> But since all Honours from inferiours flow,
> (For they doe give it; Princes doe but shew
> Whom they would have so honor'd) and that this
> On such opinions, and capacities
> Is built, as rise and fall, to more and lesse;

by striking paradox and analogy—

> If thy Prince will his subjects to call thee
> 'My Lord', and this doe swell thee, thou art then,
> By being greater, growne to bee lesse Man,

Donne shows how 'poore and lame' this life of the senses is when we
can but

> peepe through lattices of eyes, *and*
> heare through labyrinths of eares,

thus proving that happiness, beauty, honour—all that men lay store
by, are but accidental and transitory compared to the 'essentiall joy':

> The sight of God, in fulnesse . . .

This is essentiall joy, where neither hee
Can suffer diminution, nor wee . . .

Elizabeth Drury, Donne's chosen symbol of perfection, is described in
extravagant tones and imagery:

. . . she whose rich beauty lent
Mintage to other beauties . . .
Shee, in whose body . . .
The Westerne treasure, Easterne spicerie,
Europe, and Afrique, and the unknowne rest
Were easily found . . .

in order to emphasize the contrast between our present state:

. . . us slow-pac'd snailes who crawle upon
Our prisons prison, earth . . .

and what we yet will be:

When earthly bodies more celestiall
Shall be, than Angels were, for thy could fall.

The *Second Anniversary* is by no means as laboured as the *First*.
The explanation for this may be found in the sub-titles supplied by
Donne: *An Anatomie of the World* and *Of The Progresse of the Soule*.
In the *Second Anniversary* Donne has turned away from the sordid
details of the dissecting table to demonstrate to us the progress of a
soul to glory. There are some jarring notes—as in the exaggerated
image of the world as a beheaded man, or in the piling up of images
to illustrate the perfection of the resurrected spirit, which tend to con-
fuse rather than inspire, and which seem far removed from Donne's
'line of masculine expression'. Yet perhaps elsewhere in this poem
Donne could be said to combine the poet and the logical metaphysician
in almost perfect balance: as metaphysician he pursues essences, even
to the heart of ultimate reality, while his unusual but most profound
imagery proclaims the passionate thinking of the poet. His comparison
of the soul, for instance, to the pith which

Strings fast the little bones of necke and backe;
So by the Soule doth deathe string Heaven and Earth . . .

is at once original, moving and logical; while his choice of images describing death has seldom been surpassed:

> Thinke then, my soule that death is but a Groome,
> Which brings a Taper to the outward roome . . .

and again:

> . . . thinke that, but unbinding of a packe,
> To take one precious thing, thy soule from thence.

These images are significant of Donne's view of death as the gateway to true life, true reality—for

> Only in Heaven joyes strength is never spent;
> And accidentall things are permanent.

Many critics have wondered about Donne's preoccupation, both in his poems and in his sermons, with the subject of death, even in its grimmest details of 'winding sheets, tombs and worms and tumbling to decay,' particularly in his own funeral sermon, *Death's Duell*, which he preached with an almost morbid relish at Whitehall, shortly before his death. Perhaps it was that ancient childhood fear of death that lingered on subconsciously, and which Donne thought to exorcise by means of dramatic meditation, and by the bravura of posing in his shroud for the statue which stands in St. Paul's to-day, in his memory. One would have thought it more consistent with his temper to wrestle with death—to dispute its claims and the manner of its coming. Helen Gardner argues, that because the full imaginative acceptance of death as a liberation of the soul, celebrated in the *Second Anniversary*, is missing from the six Holy Sonnets concerned with Death and Judgment, these must have been written before 1612, and she suggests 1609 as an appropriate date. In these, it seems to me, Donne is more the meditative poet that Martz has championed, than the lively searcher after truth we have known in the *Songs and Sonets*, though the dialectic is still the controlling principle.

Holy Sonnet IX: 'If poysonous mineralls . . .' has however much of the true Donnean audacity and wit, and reminds one of G. M. Hopkins

in the way the emotion is conveyed by means of the broken rhythm
and the irregularly recurring caesura:

> But who am I, that dare dispute with thee,
> O God?

But the dialectic links are weak; the passion is dissipated, as Donne
seems to jump from one ground of appeal to another, with—seemingly—more regard for assembling excuses than for procuring an
answer to the riddle he first proposed: if minerals and plants and
animals cannot be damned,

> Why should I bee?
> Why should intent or reason, borne in mee,
> Make sinnes, else equall, in mee more heinous?
> And mercy being easie, and glorious
> To God; in his sterne wrath, why threatens hee?

There is a moving pathos in the final couplet:

> That thou remember them (i.e., his sins), some claime as debt,
> I thinke it mercy, if thou wilt forget,

but we miss the tension, the ambiguity, 'the anguish of the marrow',
which give an almost elemental force to his great love lyrics.

I find a similar absence of stress in the other Holy Sonnets on Death, a
labouring of the dialectic to simplify and to state the case rather than
to grapple with it and resolve it:

> As due by many titles I resigne
> Myselfe to thee, O God, first I was made
> By thee, and for thee . . .
> I am thy sonne, made with thyselfe to shine,
> Thy servant . . .
> Thy sheepe, thine Image . . .
>   *H.S. II.*

We get the same impression in *Holy Sonnet IV*, where he addresses
his soul in a series of conventional images:

> Oh my blacke Soule! . . .
> Thou art like a pilgrim . . .
> Or like a thiefe . . .

Others are more dramatic, and more lively in quality, as in *H.S. VII* where Donne's imagination is fired by his exciting vision of the Last Day:

> At the round earths imagin'd corners, blow
> Your trumpets, Angells, and arise, arise
> From death, you numberlesse infinities
> Of soules . . .;

or in *H.S. XIII*: 'What if this present were the worlds last night?' where Donne meditates on the divine mercy ensured by the picture of Christ crucified—with an oddly-touching glance back to the past:

> . . . as in my idolatrie
> I said to all my profane mistresses,
> Beauty, of pitty, foulnesse onely is
> A signe of rigour: so I say to thee,
> To wicked spirits are horrid shapes assign'd,
> This beauteous forme assures a pitious minde.

The dialectic in *H.S. V* is more close-knit and therefore more moving and more compelling—perhaps because its subject is so very close to Donne's heart:

> I am a little world made cunningly
> Of Elements, and an Angelike spright,
> But blacke sinne hath betraid to endlesse night
> My worlds both parts . . .

The imagery, taken from the new science connected with the telescope, gives new significance—almost a new dimension—to his old concept of his body as the microcosm:

> You, which beyond that heaven which was most high
> Have found new sphears, and of new lands can write,
> Powre new seas in mine eyes, that so I might
> Drowne my world with my weeping earnestly . . .

The final couplet in many of the Holy Sonnets states a truth in paradoxical form. Some are memorable, mainly because of the convincing logic of the unusual images, e.g.,

Thy Grace may wing me to prevent his art, (i.e. the devil's)
And thou like Adamant draw mine iron heart

H.S. I;

or, because of the majesty of the thought stated so succinctly:

God cloth'd him selfe in vile mens flesh, that so
Hee might be weake enough to suffer woe.

H.S. XI.

Some, however, seem forced—indeed almost melodramatic—in character, e.g.,

Or wash thee in Christs blood, which hath this might
That being red, it dyes red soules to white.

H.S. IV;

or, the couplet ending the *H.S. V*, quoted above:

And burne me O Lord, with a fiery zeale
Of thee and thy house, which doth in eating heale.

In *Holy Sonnet XIV*: 'Batter my heart . . .'—it is interesting to note how the characteristically vehement dialectic of the scholastic Donne is replaced by the equally eloquent argument of the battering-ram, which he forges out of the repetition of words describing action: batter . . . knock . . . breathe . . . shine . . . breake . . . blowe . . . burn . . . and which lends such force to the recapitulary paradox of the climax:

for I
Except you enthrall mee, never shall be free,
Nor ever chast, except you ravish mee.

Though this is one of the most dramatic of the Sonnets we still do not 'feel the thought as immediately as the odour of a rose'—to quote T. S. Eliot's noted saying. We must remember however that it is only by comparison with the pulsating passion of the *Songs and Sonets* that these sonnets suffer. When we compare them with Herbert's divine colloquies, for example, *The Collar*, we are at once aware of the more urgent and more rugged individuality of Donne's assaults upon Heaven:

Thou hast made me, and shall thy worke decay?
Repaire me now . . .

H.S. I;

or

> Spit in my face you Jewes, and pierce my side, . . .
> For I have sinn'd, and sinn'd, and onely hee,
> Who could do no iniquitie, hath dyed . . .
>
> H.S. XI;

or, lastly,

> Except thou rise and for thine owne worke fight
> Oh I shall soone despaire . . .
>
> H.S. II.

Donne, always conscious of his unworthiness, forever preoccupied with the question of his personal redemption, could never soar into the tranquil contemplative regions where Herbert and Vaughan were so at home. In the following poem he comes nearest, perhaps, to acceptance and to peace of soul.

Hymne to God My God, in My Sicknesse:

There is some difference among critics about the dating of this poem. Walton claims it was written eight days before Donne's death, in March 1631, but other students of Donne, among whom is Helen Gardner,[6] trace it to Donne's serious illness in 1623. To my mind, it is the finest of the *Divine Poems*. Though lacking the turbulence and tension, and the tenuous balance, of his best *Songs and Sonets*, it embodies the chief characteristics of our poet: the exacting dialectic controlling the whole form and development of the poem; the witty conceits, which display ever new depths in Donne's imaginative conceptions; the new learning blended with old legends; the sublimest Christian doctrine paralleled with the most precise knowledge of contemporary geographical explorations, and, leavening it all, the paradoxical wit which is so truly Donne's—the wit which enables us not only to grasp the sublime imaginative truth which is the theme of the poem, but which helps us to see, as it were, Donne's whole life in marvellous retrospect.

The first stanza declares his purpose: here on this 'bank and shoal of time' he will try to adjust his perspective:

> . . . As I come
> I tune the Instrument here at the dore . . .

---

[6] H. Gardner, *The Divine Poems*, 1952, Appendix E, pp. 132–135.

He will try to see the design in the whirling flux which was his life; to pay a last tribute to that divine order which is reflected in the marvellous system of correspondences in the Universe, and to the divine Wisdom which, ever since the Word became Flesh, speaks to us through paradox.

The basic paradox from which springs the triumphant tone of the poem is placed centrally at the end of stanza three:

> So death doth touch the Resurrection,

and is arrived at by means of the logical analogies which Donne draws between the physicians examining his sick body, and the cosmographers poring over maps, and so making the 'South-West discoverie', i.e., the straits of Magellan which join the Western world of the Atlantic to the Eastern Pacific. And he concludes with consummate assurance:

> As West and East
> In all flatt Maps (and I am one) are one,
> So death doth touch the Resurrection.

Here, once again, Donne's imagination is engaged with his favourite image of the microcosm; his body being visualized as a contracted world in which the passage from life to death, and hence to the resurrection, becomes as exciting as any of the discoveries made by the explorers of the New World.

Still pursuing analogies in the geographical sphere he puns brilliantly on the word 'straits':

> Per fretum febris, by these streights to die;

and in stanza four, his play on its double meaning lends great imaginative depth to the poem. The straits of Anyan, Magellan and Gibraltar, leading respectively to the East (the abode of Sem), to Africa (where Cham lived), and to Jerusalem (the home of Japhet), are portrayed on the material and physical level as the way to the riches and pleasures of this world, and on the supernatural level as the straits we must suffer as we journey through life towards the comprehensive happiness of the New Jerusalem. It is characteristic of Donne's keen wit to fuse in a single image precise historical and geographical facts, basic Christian doctrine, as well as his own life experience, so crossed by straits of all kinds.

In stanza five Donne reverts to the primary 'Death-Resurrection'
paradox in soaring lines, made powerful by their concentration and by
their evocation of old-time legend and traditional dogma in its elucida-
tion:

> We thinke that Paradise and Calvarie,
> Christs Crosse, and Adams tree, stood in one place.

Then, by an imaginative and logical transition, he identifies himself
with both Christ and Adam:

> Looke Lord, and finde both Adams met in me,

following it by a prayer in which acceptance and supplication,
acknowledgement of guilt and trust in God's mercy are all blended:

> As the first Adams sweat surrounds my face,
> May the last Adams blood my soule embrace.

The prayer continues into the final stanza:

> So, in his purple wrapp'd receive me Lord . . .

where we hear echoed the tremendous conceit of the Vexilla Regis:

> Arbor decora et fulgida
> Ornata Regis purpura,

Christ's blood becoming the royal purple with its promise of a kingly
pardon. Few of Donne's images have the intensity or the sublimity of
this. The perfect 'associative leap' it implies, could have taken place
only when Donne was very deeply moved. Here certainly, T. S.
Eliot's dictum is borne out:

> A thought to Donne was an experience; it modified his sensibility.[7]

His 'instrument' i.e. his soul, having been tuned by the traditional
means of self-examination, meditation and prayer, the poem ends on a
quiet Biblical note which is in keeping with the paradoxical nature
of the poem:

> Therefore that he may raise the Lord throws down.

---

[7] *Selected Prose*, ed. Hayward, 'The Metaphysical Poets', 1953, p. 117.

The ending may seem rather flat after the near-ecstasy of stanza five, but, as in *The Extasie*, it suggests the calm after the struggle, the 'port after stormie seas'. It may be significant too of the meditative evening-tide of Donne's life, when the fitful fever and the disputatious days of his youth were gone forever.

The main difference between these *Divine Poems* and the earlier *Songs and Sonets* is a difference in the degree of Donne's energy and of his passion. While the earlier poems are forged, one could say, in the passionate experience and intellectual turmoil of the living moment, the *Divine Poems* are mostly meditations on facts from which Donne's faith has never really wavered. Here I should like to refer to the brilliant thesis of Professor Martz,[8] that English religious poetry of the seventeenth century draws its main and distinctive qualities from the art of meditation i.e. a method of meditation based on the Spiritual Exercises of St. Ignatius, and introduced into England with the Counter-Reformation. According to this method, the meditation falls into three distinct parts, corresponding to the acts of memory, under-standing and will, and called respectively composition of place, analysis and colloquy. Martz examines seventeenth century religious poetry to see whether 'meditative poetry' is not a more accurate description, and does not provide a greater and more inclusive tradition for such poetry than, for example, the term 'metaphysical'.

He presumes from the circumstances of Donne's life and family that he was 'subjected to a strong Jesuit influence during his formative years', and concludes that therefore he must have been trained in this special Jesuit method of meditation. I do not see how this need neces-sarily be true. In the first place, we have no direct evidence whatever that Donne was thus 'subjected to a strong Jesuit influence'. In the second place, even if it be granted that he had a Jesuit tutor up to his eleventh year when he went on to Oxford, he would be far too young to be subjected to, and to benefit from, any such training. The art of meditation is a mature art.

It seems unlikely that he was introduced to anything so difficult as the Spiritual Exercises of St. Ignatius in his Catholic childhood,

---

[8] *The Poetry of Meditation*, 1954, p. 38.

remarks Miss Latham, but she goes on to point to the highly relevant problem:

> Where he found the threefold structure, if not in meditative technique, is a question still to be solved.[9]

It is my belief that Donne found the threefold structure of his poetry in his early training in logic at the University. One of the first objects of the course would be to introduce the student to the workings of his own mind, and to demonstrate to him its threefold operation consisting of: simple apprehension; then, judgment or analysis—where two or more concepts are examined and joined together to form a proposition; and finally, the act of reasoning, where two or more propositions are linked so as to arrive at a conclusion. That this was basic training at the Universities is borne out by the evidence of Fr. Costello who found that the logic notebooks of the seventeenth-century Cambridge students were arranged according to the threefold operation just described.[10] It is scarcely necessary to point out that the syllogism, the ancient disputation, indeed all man's thinking—including the Jesuit method of meditation—are based on this fundamental three-fold movement of the mind. Although Martz does admit that the Jesuit methods of meditation are in themselves

> adaptations of ancient principles of logic and rhetoric,

and that they develop the natural tendency of the human mind to work from a particular concept or situation, through analysis and judgment to a resolution of the problems presented, he still insists on giving priority of influence to the Ignatian meditation, seeing it as the

> fundamental organizing impulse deep within the poetry.[11]

Martz carefully analyses a number of *Holy Sonnets* and *Divine Poems*, showing in each case, how they adhere to the meditative pattern. Thus in *Goodfriday, 1613*, he demonstrates the division of the poem into three parts:

[9] A. M. C. Latham, *The Year's Work in Eng. Studies*, 1961, p. 158.
[10] W. T. Costello, *Scholastic Curriculum at Early 17th C. Cambridge*, 1958, p. 47.
[11] *The Poetry of Meditation*, op. cit., pp. 38, 39.

Lines 1-10: The composition of place by means of similitudes, setting
  the problem precisely;
Lines 11-32: The exercise of the understanding, in the intellectual
  analysis of what Martz calls 'the paradox of human perversity';
Lines 33-42: The exercise of the will in the Ignatian colloquy.

From evidence such as this he concludes that these poems

> are, in the most specific sense of the term, meditations, Ignatian
> meditations: providing strong evidence for the profound impact
> of early Jesuit training upon the later career of J. Donne.[12]

His analyses certainly prove that there are parallel movements in the
poems and in the meditations—but is there not a more fundamental
influence transcending and antedating both genres? From a study of
the sixteenth century curriculum at Oxford and its influence on Donne
—as well as on the men of letters of his day—would it not seem to
follow that his training in logic and dialectic was more fundamental
as regards the structure of his thought, and hence of his poems, than
any influence from a system, which, when all is said and done, is itself
based upon the same basic logical principles—the principles of thought
itself? The Jesuit method of meditation—particularly as treated in the
Continental works of the Counter-Reformation to which Martz
makes so much reference—would then appear not as the 'fundamental
organizing impulse deep within the poetry', but as a new stimulus,
particularly with regard to Donne's *Divine Poems* which, though controlled as all his poems are by the dialectic method, are distinctly
meditative in character.

   Having remarked on the main difference between the Divine Poems
and Donne's earlier *Sonets*, *Elegies* and *Satyres*, it is necessary to stress
once again the fact that their fundamental resemblance is greater. From
the early days of *Satyre III*, with its vision of Truth on the cragged hill
top, and its symbolic and prophetic lines:

> . . . hee that will
> Reach her, about must, and about must goe,

Donne's unceasing search has been for that truth, that ultimate reality,
which he felt was hidden somewhere, permanently, behind the flux

---

[12] *The Poetry of Meditation*, op. cit., p. 54.

and fashions of life, beneath the smug complacency, or the fears and the deceits of his own conscience, beyond the glitter of 'things extreme and scattering bright', within the essence of all that is

> 'prized and passes of us, everything that's fresh and fast-flying of us';

the One that is at once the Cause, the Being, and the consummation of the Many.

In his secular Songs and in his *Divine Poems*, as well as in his prose works, meditations, letters and sermons, Donne was first and last a man with a great hunger for God.

> Keepe the lively tast you hold of God—

his advice in a *Verse Letter* to his friend, Sir Henry Goodyer,[13] is but a reflection of his own living faith.

> In heaven, at last, all things should ebbe back into God, as all things flowed from Him at first, and so there should be no other Essence but God . . .[14]

One could say of Donne with perfect truth, that he would not have so persistently sought for the real and permanent, the Essence in the heart of things, if he had not already found it. Note the significance of the implication here:

> In what torne ship soever I embarke,
> That ship shall be my embleme of thy Arke . . .;

and the sublime confession in the lines:

> As the trees sap doth seeke the root below
> In winter, in my winter now I goe,
> Where none but thee, th' Eternall root
> Of true Love I may know.
>
> from *A Hymne to Christ*

---

[13] *Poetry & Prose*, Hayward, p. 155.
[14] 'Fifty Sermons', 29, quoted by I. Husain in *Dogmatic & Mystical Theology of Donne*, 1938, p. 114.

'. . . I'll
Have an eye to the sakes of him, quaint moonmarks, to his pelted
plumage under
Wings.'

G. M. Hopkins: *Henry Purcell*

CONCLUSION

It is significant that students of Donne down the years seem to have had as much difficulty in arriving at a balanced assessment of his genius, as he himself had in achieving a balance in his personal life between the warring elements of his rich nature.

The simple, but nevertheless perceptive picture that Walton first drew of Donne as the 'second Augustine' has long since been considered as altogether too flattering and too naïve for the writers who come with more scholarly detachment it is true, but also perhaps more interested in the particular literary theses they wish to prove, than in attempting to discover the truth about Donne, through the totality of his work and the deeply personal expression of himself in his poetry. Thus the pendulum of his criticism has swung with varying momentum from the extreme of concentration on the man himself, resulting in a sub-jective reading of his poetry, to the other extreme of a one-sided pre-occupation with the details of his craft, which, stripping it of its flesh and blood, its passion, left us only with the dry bones of his imagery or with samples of the shock tactics of his dramatic method.

From the extreme of Dr. Johnson's comments on the violent yoking together of the images used by Donne, we are brought by Gosse to an absorption with the enigmatic rebel, and the end-of-the-century emphasis on Donne, the Hamlet-like skeptic and melancholic. Grier-son's classic edition of Donne's poems in 1912, together with his masterly commentary, redressed the balance, and provided the basis for a more realistic approach to the study of the poet, by stressing what are undoubtedly the dominant characteristics of his love poetry: the strains of dialectic and of vivid realism. From Grierson's time on the pendulum has tended to swing more and more away from pre-occupation with Donne the man, to a greater interest in the details of his method, the analysis of his art, the peculiarities of his thought. Yet, here again, we meet with extreme views on Donne: Miss Ramsay's conception of him[1] as the confirmed medievalist and schol-astic, opposed by Courthope's championing of him as the first of the moderns[2]; T. S. Eliot's classifying of the contents of the poems as 'sensuous thoughts' indicating a unified sensibility, balanced by some fine critics of Donne's method and craft such as Legouis, Leishman,

---

[1] M. P. Ramsay: *Les Doctrines Medievales chez Donne*, 1917.
[2] W. J. Courthope: *History of English Poetry*, 1903.

Helen Gardner and Martz. It is not too fanciful, I think, to imagine Donne taunting us, Hamlet-fashion, across the centuries:

> You would pluck out the heart of my mystery; you would sound me from my lowest note to the top of my compass . . . (but) though you can fret me, you cannot play upon me . . .

We have to ask ourselves what is the 'heart of his mystery'? Wherein lies the ultimate individualizing essence, the 'haecceitas', the 'thisness' of Donne's genius, particularly as it reveals itself in his poetry, and which distinguishes him from all other poets? It cannot lie alone in the dialectical structure of his verse nor in his method of logical reasoning, for in this wide domain many other poets have claims. Poets from Wm. Dunbar to Thomas Nashe frequently employed a perceptible logical basis for their poems, and the sonnets of Wm. Alabaster (1568–1640) show a definite dialectical teasing of the subject. Later on we find that though Sir Philip Sidney's sonnets (see especially Sonnets LIII and LIX) are highly dramatic and aerated by a kind of witty exaggeration, they yet follow perfectly logical arguments. Still, no one could mistake the earth-bound and sometimes plodding dialectic of the early poets, or the courtly tone of Sidney's gallant arguments, for the verve, the piquancy, the intensity and energy of Donne's mind as it flashed, meteor-like from notion to analogy without ever losing the track of his argument in this dialectical 'tour de force'.

Besides, the dialectical method has been employed by other metaphysical poets, notably by Marvell, who is, as regards structure and method, Donne's superior. There is nothing in the vehement dialectic of the *Songs and Sonets* to compare with the cool logic and the urbane, syllogistic reasoning of *To his Coy Mistress*, or with the conciseness and the ease with which the argument is sustained in *The Definition of Love*. The difference between Donne and Marvell is deeper than can be measured by comparing their methods of structure, the build-up of their syllogisms, or indeed, their whole conduct of the dialectical game.

The poems of Marvell are written, we feel, *after* the event, when the heat of the argument has cooled, and the poet can write about his problem in a detached and therefore more controlled manner. There is no straining to attain a 'modus vivendi' between the rival claimants of body and soul, matter and spirit; no 'naked thinking heart' to upset the order of the dialectic or to betray the poet in his inmost citadel. We are conscious of the cool tact, the reserve, allowing us to intrude so far and no farther; the graciousness through which we are invited to hear the judge's dispassionate summing up of the case, but not to embroil ourselves in the hard-hitting and uncertain fray.

With Donne, as we have seen throughout this study, the case is very different. Reading his poems is like a living experience; we feel that we are taking part in a real argument, wary of being trapped by its sophisms, bracing ourselves for its tensions, puzzled by its ambiguities, uncertain of its resolution. And here I think, we touch on the heart of Donne's mystery. For Donne's problems there could be no resolution on earth; they stretch out into infinity, teasing the mind to the limits of its capacity, taxing the heart and senses with mysteries beyond their reach, experiences which have in them something of the transcendental. It is not the dialectical slant of his mind which sets Donne apart from other poets; it is not the wit of his arguments nor the strangeness of his conceits. That which distinguishes him is the urgency of the passion pulsating through the dialectic, transforming it, even from the early days of *Satyre III*, from a dusty and coldly-correct academic exercise, into a deeply personal search for the truth; a passionate analysis of reality—not just physical or material reality—but that metaphysical reality which has its expression in man's own composite being, in all his conscious states of thinking and feeling, particularly in the intimate psychosomatic relationship of human love, and which can have its dénouement only in the ultimate, synthesising Cause of reality, the very Ground of our being, the Creator Himself. It is essentially in this sense that Donne can claim to be a 'metaphysical' poet. Aristotle who gave to metaphysics its classical object points out that it is

> . . . a science which investigates being as being, and the attributes which belong to this in virtue of its own nature . . .
>
> *Metaphysics*, Bk. IV, Chap. I

Being is but a synonym for reality; and if we look upon reality as an expression of the Divine Essence we can understand the eternal desire of the human soul to possess, to be at one with the real. This desire Donne had to an intense degree all his life long.

The thing to wonder at in him is, not that which has been stressed so often—his conversion from the gay Jack Donne of the *Songs and Sonets* and the *Elegies*, to the saintly Dr. Donne of the *Divine Poems* and the Sermons—but rather the unchanging nature of the man. Youthful ideals and mottoes are very frequently the outward sign of that inward essence which is the potent principle of individuality.

Viewed in this light the Spanish motto on Donne's earliest portrait, taken before he had reached his twentieth year, is most significant:

'Antes muerto que mudado': sooner dead than changed.[3]

Just as a wheel has its meaning by the convergence of its parts on its centre, so Donne's life and his personal expression through the dialectic of his works, have meaning by their convergence on the very core of reality—the Being which explains all being, and the Standard from which all values spring. God alone is the ultimate reality. Everything else—person or thing—made by Him, is real, and therefore good, when it is true to its own divinely appointed nature, when, as Hopkins puts it, it 'deals out that being indoors each one dwells'. Reality thus reflects the divine order in creation, so that if a man accepts his manhood and is rightly orientated towards God, and towards things and people, he will possess a balanced outlook which will never be shocked by anything in the human situation. It is not reality but unreality which is to be feared, because it is a negation of life itself and therefore of God, without values and without order.

A healthy attitude towards life, towards reality, helps to peel off the crust formed on man's sensibility by custom or convention, or by the clichés of an unreal society. As Screwtape remarks, it makes him feel 'that he is coming home, recovering himself.'[4] Donne's hunger for what was real and true was at once the saving grace and the motive force of his life.

His richly gifted and highly sensitive nature was, as we have seen in Chapter I, the battleground in which he sought to reconcile the diversities of his being: the craving of his bodily senses for satisfaction, of his heart for love, and of his mind and soul for union with that which transcended sense experience, yet included and explained it in a deeper vision. The more conscious Donne was of the dichotomies within, in his case aggravated by the divided loyalties of his personal life, the more he sought for a stable criterion of truth, an ultimate unifying force: the One amongst the many, who could explain and give significance to the diversities within his being and experience.

One can see how suited the dialectical method was to such a nature

---

[3] T. E. Terrill, *MLN*, XLIII, 1928, p. 318.
  He traces the verse to Montemayor's *Diana* and shows that they are the words which Diana wrote on the sand, in pledging her troth to Sirenus.

[4] C. S. Lewis, *The Screwtape Letters*, 1942, pp. 49 and 68.

11

since opposition and tension are the life of dialectic, providing the dynamism which seeks by means of analysis and analogy, a synthesis of the seemingly incompatible, an acceptable if precarious balance of reality.

In all this one is reminded so strongly of St. Augustine that one's respect grows for Walton, who was the first to pin-point the resemblance. Book X of the *Confessions* could have been written by Donne. (See Appendix B).

At the end of this Book, in a passionate cry which sums up Donne's as well as Augustine's life-long quest, we read:

> . . . where I found Truth, there found I my
> God, the Truth itself . . .

> Too late have I loved Thee . . .
> And behold, Thou wert within, and I abroad, and
> there I searched for Thee . . .

> When I shall with my whole self cleave to Thee,
> I shall no where have sorrow, or labour; and my
> life shall wholly live, as wholly full
> of Thee.[5]

Perhaps we could allow the pendulum to swing back a little; to infuse into our present day studies connected with Donne's method and art, and the interpretation of his poems against the background of his times, a little of the intuitive appreciation accorded him in the early tributes paid by men such as Walton, his first biographer, and Carew, the composer of one of his earliest elegies. It is significant that the first quality to which Carew draws our attention is Donne's passionate and flaming spirit:

> . . . But the flame
> Of thy brave soule, (that shot such heat and light,
> As burnt our earth, and made our darknesse bright,
> Committed holy rapes upon our will . . .
> And the deeper knowledge of darke truths so teach,
> As sense might judge, what phansie could not reach;)
> Must be desir'd for ever. So the fire,
> That fills with spirit and heat the Delphique quire,

---

[5] *The Confessions of St. Augustine*, trans. E. B. Pusey, 1929, pp. 208–227.

Which kindled first by thy Promethean breath,
Glow'd here a while . . .[6]

In 1828, De Quincey praised Donne for his combination of:

the last sublimation of dialectical subtlety and address with the most impassioned majesty,[7]

while at the end of the century—in 1896—Saintsbury also pays tribute to what he calls Donne's 'flower of incandescence'. Quoting Bossuet: 'Nos passions ont quelque chose d'infini', he goes on to say in connection with Donne:

To express infinity no doubt is a contradiction in terms. But no poet has gone nearer to the hinting and adumbration of this infinite quality of passion, and of the relapses and reactions from passion, than the author of *The Second Anniversary* . . . and *The Extasie*.[8]

It is indeed 'the passion and the life whose fountains are within' which give to the dialectic of Donne's verse, and to the soaring sentences of his sermons, the dynamic quality, the vibrant sincerity, and the characteristic energy which make them uniquely his. Grierson rightly remarks that:

poems are not written by influences or movements or sources, but come from the living hearts of men.[9]

*   *   *

'In its point of completion,' remarks Kreyche, 'metaphysics takes us beyond the realities of sense; yet in its point of origin metaphysics begins (where all human knowledge begins) in the observed realities of sense.'[10]

---

[6] T. Carew, 'An Elegie upon the death of Dr. John Donne', *The Metaphysical Poets*, ed. H. Gardner, p. 141.
[7] *The Collected Writings of Thomas De Quincey*, ed. David Masson, 1890, Vol. X, 'Essay on Rhetoric, p. 101.
[8] *Poems of John Donne*, ed. Sir E. K. Chambers with Intro. by G. Saintsbury, 1896, p. xxxiii.
[9] H. J. C. Grierson, *Metaphysical Lyrics & Poems of 17th C.* 'Donne to Butler', 1921, p. xvii.
[10] P. J. Kreyche, *First Philosophy*, N. Y., 1959, p. 27.

That is where Donne's metaphysical quest began—in true Aristotelian and Thomistic fashion—in the things of sense, in the reality of his own human nature and of his emotional and intellectual experiences, particularly in the deeply personal experience of human love. One could say that he was by nature orientated towards the spiritual and the eternal which belong to the essence of all things. Even in the year of his greatest disillusionment, 1601, he could say with confidence:

> For though through many streights, and lands I roame,
> I launch at paradise, and I saile towards home.
>
> *The Progresse of the Soule.*

What Donne was doing, in actual as in literary fact, through all the mazes of his dialectical search, through his passionate straining after wholeness of being, and through the long 'anguish of the marrow' was, in the words of C. S. Lewis:

> coming home, recovering himself

for the reality and the truth which he sought were at once the essence and the ultimate Source of all Being.

BIBLIOGRAPHY

Abbreviations:

KR: Kenyon Review
MLR: Modern Language Review
HR: Hudson Review
PQ: Philological Quarterly
RES: Review of English Studies
MP: Modern Philology
MLN: Modern Language Notes

Works of John Donne:

DONNE, J., *Pseudo-Martyr*, 1610.
    Essays in Divinity, published by Donne's son, 1651.
    Letters to Severall Persons of Honour, published by Donne's son, 1651.
    Devotions upon Emergent Occasions, ed. J.H.A. Sparrow, 1923.
Poems of John Donne, ed. Chambers, E.K., Vol. I, 1896.
Life and Letters of J. Donne, ed. Gosse, E., 1899.
The Poems of J. Donne, ed. Grierson, H.J.C., Vol. II, 1912.
Complete Poetry and Selected Prose, ed. Hayward, J., 1945.
Donne's Sermons, ed. Smith, L.P., 1919.

General:

ADAMSON, R., *Short History of Logic*, 1911.
ALVAREZ, A., *The School of Donne*, 1961.
AQUINAS, ST. THOMAS, *Summa Contra Gentiles*, trans. J. Rickaby, 1905.
    Aquinas Ethicus, trans. J. Rickaby, 1896.
ARISTOTLE, *The Nicomachean Ethics*, trans. R.W. Browne, 1853.
AUGUSTINE, ST., *The Confessions*, trans. E.B. Pusey, 1929.
BENNET, J., 'The Love Poetry of J. Donne' in *Seventeenth Century Studies Presented to Sir H. Grierson*, 1938.
BETHELL, S.L., *Gracian, Tesauro & The Nature of Metaphysical Wit*, 1953.
BREDVOLD, L.I., *The Religious Thought of Donne*, 1925.
BROOKS, CLEANTH, *The Well Wrought Urn*, edd. 1947, 1949.
BUSH, DOUGLAS, 'Science and Literature' in *Seventeenth Century Science and the Arts*, ed. H.H. Rhys, 1961.
CHARDIN, T. DE, *Le Milieu Divin*, Fontana Bks., 1964.
CHESTERTON, G.K., *St. Thomas Aquinas*, 1938.
CLAUDEL, P., *Positions et Propositions*, 1928.
COFFIN, C.M., *J. Donne and the New Philosophy*, 1937.
COLERIDGE, S.T., Biographia Literaria. ed. G. Watson, 1956.
    Coleridge's Miscellaneous Criticism, ed. J.M. Raysor, 1936.
COSTELLO, W.T., *The Scholastic Curriculum at early Seventeenth Century Cambridge*, 1958.
COURTHOPE, W.J., *The History of English Poetry*, 1903.
CRAIG, H., *The Enchanted Glass*, 1952.

CROFTS, J.E.V., 'J. Donne: A Reconsideration' in *Twentieth Century Views*, ed. H. Gardner, 1962.

CURTIS, M.H., *Oxford and Cambridge in Transition*, 1959.

DRUMMOND, W., *Conversations with Drummond of Hawthornden*, ed. R.F. Patterson. 1923.
The Works of Drummond of Hawthornden, 1711.

ELIOT, T.S.E., 'Donne in Our Time': *A Garland for J. Donne*, ed. T. Spencer, Harvard U.P., 1931.
'Andrew Marvell': *Selected Essays*, 1949.
Selected Prose, ed. J. Hayward, 1953.

EMPSON, W., 'Donne and the Rhetorical Tradition', *KR*, Autumn, 1949.
Seven Types of Ambiguity, 1961.

GARDNER, H., *The Divine Poems*, 1952.
'An Interpretation of Aire and Angels' in *The Business of Criticism*, 1959.
'The Argument about the Extasie' in *Elizabethan and Jacobean Studies Presented to F.P. Wilson*, 1959.
The Metaphysical Poets (Penguin).

GILBEY, T., *Barbara Celarent: A Description of Scholastic Dialectic*, 1949.

GILSON, E., *The Spirit of Medieval Philosophy*, 1950.
Painting and Reality, 1958.

GRAVES, F.P., *P. Ramus and the Educational Reformation of the 16th Century*, 1912.

GRIERSON, H.J.C., 'Donne': *Cambridge History of English Literature*, Vol. iv, 1909.
Metaphysical Lyrics and Poems of Seventeenth Century, 'Donne to Butler', 1921.
Background of English Literature, 1934.

HOWELL, W.S., *Logic and Rhetoric in England, 1500–1700*, 1956.

HUGHES, Merritt, 'The Lineage of the Extasie' *MLR*, Jan. 1932, No. 1.

HUNT, C., *Donne's Poetry*, Yale U.P., 1954.

HUSAIN, I., *Dogmatic and Mystical Theology of Donne*, 1938.

JOHNSON, S., *Lives of the Poets*, ed. G. Birkbeck-Hill, 1896.

KEAST, W.R. (ed.) *Seventeenth Century English Poetry*, 1962.

KER, W.P., *On Modern Literature*, 1956.

KERMODE, F., *J. Donne*, 1957.

KOESTLER, A., *The Sleepwalkers*, 1959.

KREYCHE, R.J., *First Philosophy*, N.Y., 1959.

KROOK, D., *Three Traditions of Moral Thought*, 1959.

LATHAM, A.M.C., *The Year's Work in English Studies*, 1961.

LEAVIS, F.R., *Revaluation*, 1936.

LEGOUIS, P., *Donne The Craftsman*, 1928.

LEISHMAN, J.B., *The Monarch of Wit*, 1951 and 1962.

LEWIS, C.S., 'Donne and Love Poetry in the Seventeenth Century' in *Seventeenth Century Studies Presented to H.J.C. Grierson*, 1938.
The Four Loves, 1960.
The Screwtape Letters, 1942.

MALLET, C.E., *History of the University of Oxford*, 1924.

McLUHAN, H.M., 'Tradition and the Academic Talent' *HR*, Vol. i, No. 2, 1948.

MARTZ, L.L., *The Poetry of Meditation*, 1954.

MAZZEO, J.A., *Renaissance and Seventeenth Century Studies*, 1964.

MILLER, P., *The New English Mind: Seventeenth Century*, 1939.

MOLONEY, M.F., J. *Donne: His Flight from Mediaevalism*, 1944.

MORISON, S.E., *The Founding of Harvard College*, 1930.

NELSON, N.E., 'P. Ramus and the Confusion of Logic, Rhetoric and Poetry', *The University of Michigan Contributions in Mod. Philology*, No. 2, April, 1947.

ONG, W.J., 'Wit and Mystery', *Speculum* – Journ. of Medieval Studies, XXII, No. 3, 1947.
Method, Ramus and the Decay of Dialogue, Harvard U.P., 1958.

POTTER, G.R., 'Donne's Extasie Contra Legouis' *PQ*, XV, No. 3, 1936.

PRAZ, MARIO, 'Donne's Relation to the Poetry of His Time' in *A Garland for J. Donne*, Ed. T. Spencer, 1931.

RAMSAY, M.P., *Les Doctrines Médiévales chez Donne*, 1924.

RYAN, L.P., *Roger Ascham*, 1963.

SAINTSBURY, G., 'Introduction' to Chambers' edition of Donne's *Poems*, 1896.

SKELTON, R., 'Elizabethan Poetry': *Stratford-Upon-Avon Studies*, 2. 1960.

SLEIGHT, R., 'The Nocturnall': *Interpretations*, ed. J. Wain, 1955.

SMITH, A.J., 'An Examination of some Claims for Ramism', *RES*, Vol. VII. No. 28, Oct., 1956.
'The Metaphysic of Love' *RES*, Nov. 1958.

TATE, A., *On the Limits of Poetry*, N.Y., 1948.

TERRILL, T.E., *MLN*, XLIII, 1928 (On Donne's early reading).

TILLYARD, E.M.W., *The Metaphysical Poets and Milton*, 1956.

TUVE, ROSEMOND, *Elizabethan and Metaphysical Imagery*, 1947.

UNGER, L., *Donne's Poetry and Modern Criticism*, Chicago, 1950.

VANN, GERALD, *The Heart of Man*, 1943.

WALTON, I., *Walton's Lives*, 'Life of Dr. J. Donne', edd. 1670, 1903.

WATSON, G., 'Ramus, Tuve and the New Petromachia', *MP*, Vol. LV, No. 4, May, 1958.

WHITE, H.C., J. *Donne and the Psychology of Spiritual Effort*, 1951.

WILEY, M.L., 'Donne and the Poetry of Scepticism' *Hibbert Journal*, Vol. XLVIII, Jan. 1950.

WILLEY, BASIL, *The Seventeenth Century Background*, 1962.

APPENDIX A

'The lover knocks at the door of the Beloved, and a voice replies from within: "Who is there?" "It is I", he said; and the voice replied: "There is not room for thee and me in this house." And the door remained shut. Then the lover retired to a desert, and fasted and prayed in solitude. After a year he came back, and knocked once more at the door. Once more the voice asked: "Who is there?" He replied: "It is thyself". And the door opened to him.'

from *Prayer and Poetry* by M. J. Bremond, 1927.

APPENDIX B

In Book X of *The Confessions*, St. Augustine having questioned the sea and the deeps, the high heavens and the living creatures, and all the delights of sense in search of his God, comes finally to the questioning of himself:

> I turned myself unto myself . . . And behold, in me there present themselves to me soul and body, one without, the other within. By which of these ought I to seek my God. I had sought Him in the body from earth to heaven so far as I could send messengers, the beams of mine eyes. But the better is the inner, for to it as presiding and judging, all the bodily messengers reported the answers of heaven and earth, and all things therein, who said, 'we are not God, but He made us.' These things did my inner man know by the ministry of the outer: I, the inner, knew them; I, the mind, through the senses of my body . . .

Again and again like a repeated echo come the words:

> Where shall I find thee?

and then the deeply significant fact—for Donne as for Augustine:

> And how shall I find Thee, if I remember Thee not?

The Confessions of St. Augustine, trans. E. B. Pusey, 1929, pp. 208–227.

INDEX

Abelard, 35, 54.

Adamson, R., 44, 45.

Aire and Angels, 10, 117–119, 122,

Alcuin, 35.

Alvarez, A., 64, 117.

Anagram, The, 111, 112.

Anglican Church, 9, 16, 17, 85, 134.

Anniversarie, The, 130, 131.

Anti-Romantic bias, 26–31.

Apparition, The, 11.

Aquinas, St. Thomas, 75, 87, 88, 112, 115.

Aristotle, 9, 20, 35, 37, 39–42, 44–50, 53, 54, 81–84, 87–89, 112–114, 119, 154.

Ascham, R., 45.

Augustine, St., 75, 112–115, 152, 156.

Baite, The, 27.

Bennett, Mrs. J., 115, 118, 120.

Bethell, S. L., 49, 52.

Biathanatos, 8, 17, 60.

Blossome, The, 10, 11–14, 27, 81.

Bracelet, The, 78, 79.

Breake of Day, 27.

Brooks, C., 132.

Browne, Sir Thomas, 101, 108.

Bush, D., 21.

Calme, The, 62.

Campion, T., 8, 54, 136.

Canonization, The, 10, 56, 65, 66, 85, 130.

Carew, T., 25, 26, 62, 89, 156, 157.

Case, John, 43.

Chardin, T. de, 59, 60, 63, 77.

Claudel, P., 60, 87.

Coffin, C. M., 36, 53, 54.

Coleridge, S. T., 71, 119, 127.

Communitie, 27, 52.

Copernican Theory, 21, 22, 30.

Costello, W. T., 36–39, 47–51, 53–55, 84, 119, 148.

Courthope, W. J., 20, 152.

Craig, H., 36, 37, 40, 43, 48, 50, 81.

Crofts, J. E. V., 118.

Curse, The, 55.

Curtis, M. H., 21, 35–39, 44–46, 54.

Dampe, The, 81.

Death, theme of, 104, 105, 135, 140–142.

De Quincey, T., 127. 157.

Devotions Upon Emergent Occasions, 38, 76, 103, 104, 107.

Disputations at Oxford, 9, 21, 39, 53–57.

Divine Poems:

  Corona, La, 74.

  Crosse, The, 77.

  First Anniversary, The, 17, 22, 77, 88, 95–98, 136.

  Good Friday, Riding Westward, 76, 148, 149.

  Hymne to Christ, A, 60, 150.

  Hymne to God my God in My Sicknesse, A, 144–147.

  Hymne to God the Father, A, 78.

  Litanie, The, 84–86.

  Second Anniversary, The, 17, 49, 136–140, 157.

Drummond of Hawthornden, W., 25, 61, 95, 96.

Dryden, J., 128.

Ebreo, Leone, 121.

Elegies:

  Anagram, The, 111, 112.

  Bracelet, The, 78, 79.

  Comparison, The, 29.